# ON THE

# WAY

## TO SALVATION

NICLAS LJUNG

*On the way – to salvation*
*Originally published in Swedish by Libris Media 2022*

Illustration: Isac Ljung (Jonatan Knutes – original cover in Swedish)
Photo: Katie McBroom (Unsplash)

Publisher: BoD · Books on Demand, Östermalmstorg 1,
114 42 Stockholm, Sweden, bod@bod.se
Print: Libri Plureos GmbH, Friedensallee 273, 22763 Hamburg,
Germany

ISBN: 978-91-8080-927-6

# Content

# Preface

During my years as a pastor, I have met many who eagerly set out, with hopeful hearts, on a journey with Jesus Christ. They have been both young and old and have come from a wide variety of cultural backgrounds. Yet, I must admit that a quiet, persistent question has often lingered at the back of my mind: Will their faith endure, or will it fade away? I know I am not alone in carrying the painful awareness that a newly awakened faith can be both fragile and vulnerable. Perhaps this vulnerability is felt most deeply when it is a family member or close friend who loses their faith and strays from the road to salvation. Over time, I have become increasingly convinced of one thing: we must do everything we can to nurture a faith that endures, not only in moments of joy, but also through seasons of doubt and silence. For as we gently guide others, we too are shaped and strengthened on our own journey with God.

To better understand this, I find it helpful to think of the Christian faith as a journey. For most of us, that's not an unfamiliar way of thinking about life. You've probably said things like, "It's a dead end," or "I took one step forward and two steps back." Maybe you've also said, "Let's get moving," or "We're stepping into the unknown." In English, we often speak of the *way* we live, or of how we shouldn't go down certain *roads*. And we're not alone in this; many cultures around the world use similar expressions. As we'll see throughout this book, this kind of language also appears in the Bible. Both the

Old and New Testaments convey the idea that we are on a journey through life, and that life itself *is* a journey.

When I worked as a children's and youth pastor in the Swedish town of Falun, the camps we held at Dalagården were among the highlights of the year. I remember one warm and sunny summer's day when we took the youth ten kilometers deep into the forest. We left them there with water, a map, and a compass and simply said, "See you back at camp!" On the way back, they had to climb steep hills and make their way through a forest without clear paths. Along the route, they encountered checkpoints with various activities. The slowest group returned nearly seven hours later, but in high spirits. At some stations, other groups had tried to bribe the leaders for a ride back when their legs were tired or their feet sore. Even though some of the youth thought it was the hardest thing they had ever done, and others thought it was the most fun, everyone had something to talk about that evening. Those who had stayed behind soon realized they had missed out on something memorable and special. I must admit, albeit reluctantly, that the challenge might have been a bit too tough, as it truly tested the teenagers' endurance and patience.

In a similar way, if we compare life to a journey, we sometimes feel like giving up, or like finding shortcuts. At other times, we simply enjoy walking along peaceful, winding paths. But no matter how life unfolds, giving up is never an option. We all know that the journey of life can be hard. The secret to a meaningful life, then, is not choosing the easiest path, but the right one. And this is where God enters the picture. He created us, He knows why He did so, and for that reason, it is only with Him that our lives can find true meaning and purpose.

I am the first to admit that I often need help in my walk with God. There is so much in my life that God needs to transform, and like everyone else, I am not where I should be. Sometimes I run away from responsibility, other times I might withhold the truth if it will benefit me. From time to time, I may be driven by greed, convenience or self-reliance. Too often I get angry and blame others when I really should be angry at myself. I disappoint others when I fail to keep my promises, and I don't always manage to prioritize my family the way I should. Looking in the mirror, I can see that I am lacking much of the fruit of the Spirit, love, joy, peace, forbearance, kindness, goodness, faithfulness, gentleness, and self-control (Galatians 5:22–23). But at the same time, I am not as I once was, I am confident of this, that He who began a good work in me will carry it on to completion until the day of Christ Jesus (Philippians 1:6), but for now I am far from complete. We are all on a journey where God longs more than anything else to shape us, guide us and transform us into the likeness of his son Jesus Christ.

The more I read the Bible through the lens of a journey, the more I find this theme throughout the scriptures. We can read how "Enoch walked faithfully with God" (Genesis 5:24). "Noah was a righteous man, blameless among the people of his time, and he walked faithfully with God" (Genesis 6:9). Abraham was called to leave his home and go to a new land that God would show him, so he set out on a long journey to a place he did not know (Genesis 12:1-9). When the people of Israel, under the leadership of Moses, left Egypt 400 years after Abraham, it was the beginning of a journey that would take them 40 years. They wandered through deserts and the wilderness and in many ways, this came to shape the nation of Israel, and it gave them an identity as a journeying people. To commemorate this journey, the Jewish people annually celebrate the Feast of Tabernacles when they sleep in simple huts under an open sky. The unwilling prophet Jonah was called by God to go all the way to the great city of Nineveh in Assyria. In Micah we learn that God want us: "To act justly and to love mercy and to walk humbly with your God" (Micah 6:8).

Mary and Joseph later set out on a journey from Nazareth in Galilee to David's city of Bethlehem, south of Jerusalem. They were then forced to flee to Egypt in order to escape Herod's wrath (Luke 2:4, Matthew 2:13). When Jesus called his disciples, it was with the classic words "Come, follow me!" (Matthew 4:19). As I have started to see this theme throughout the Bible, I am now convinced that we must recapture this language of a journey to better understand God's plan and purpose for our lives. This way of viewing our lives will better equip us to handle our walk of faith and prepare us for the things that we are going to meet on our journey through life.

The book that you hold in your hands is the result of a life as a pastor and through a life spent together with Jesus Christ. I have seen and met many people journeying on their way through life, some of them have been passing through the valley of shadow of death, others have got themselves lost in their pursuit of their own happiness and success. This book is therefore written with several purposes in mind.

*First*, I want to help those who are new to the faith to get a good start on their walk with God. A good start is crucial to how the rest of the journey will be. The Christian life is a daily walk, step by step, day by day, on and on.

*Secondly*, I want to help those of us who are already walking with Jesus to continue to walk in all the good works which God has prepared in advance for us to do. Let us not settle at the crossroad where the road of convenience meets the road of comfort, but let us instead, move on!

*Thirdly*, this book is of a theological nature, meaning that it describes who God is. Therefore, it will help you to deepen your understanding of the life that God has called us to live. For me, who view myself as a charismatic, missional, evangelical Baptist, there are two authorities on which I base my theology. First, I have the Bible which is the word of God through the words of men in history. When we read the Bible under the guidance of the Holy Spirit, with an understanding of what the text meant to its first readers, we get the correct picture of God and his will. Secondly there is the authority of Jesus Christ, the Son of God, who embodies God and reveals the Father to us. This Jesus, whom the New Testament describes, gives us knowledge of who God is, and what He is like. If you want to know God, then look at Jesus. Therefore, the Bible as a whole, is our ultimate authority for life and doctrine provides we read it in light of history and with the guidance and revelation of the Holy Spirit. It is my firm belief that we need to constantly return to the Bible to get answers to the questions that we may face as humanity. I want us to constantly live with the attitude of, "What does God's word say?" We need to read the Bible in its context, where God, from the dawn of creation until Christ's return, reveals the full redemptive story.

Finally, my longing and prayer is that this book will help both new and old travelers to gain a deeper understanding of the life that God calls us to walk and that our love of Jesus will grow.

Some final words before you start to read. You can read this book as you would read any other book, but I recommend that you read it as a part of your daily devotion. Let the words sink in and reflect over them during the day, talk to your friends about them or read this book together in a small group. In order that you don't read too much in one day I have divided the book into smaller portions marked with flags.

In Swedish there is also a small group material available. 12 shorter films each six to seven minutes long. They are subtitled into English, Farsi and some other languages. Website: www.pavag.info

This is an extended translation of the book *På väg – med frälsningen som mål*, with some additional content added.

God bless you on your journey, on the way to salvation.

/ Niclas Ljung Malmö 2024

For this reason, since the day we heard about you, we have not stopped praying for you. We continually ask God to fill you with the knowledge of his will through all the wisdom and understanding that the Spirit gives, so that you may live a life worthy of the Lord and please him in every way: bearing fruit in every good work, growing in the knowledge of God, being strengthened with all power according to his glorious might so that you may have great endurance and patience, and giving joyful thanks to the Father, who has qualified you to share in the inheritance of his holy people in the kingdom of light.

For he has rescued us from the dominion of darkness and brought us into the kingdom of the Son he loves, in whom we have redemption, the forgiveness of sins.

The Son is the image of the invisible God, the firstborn over all creation. For in him all things were created: things in heaven and on earth, visible and invisible, whether thrones or powers or rulers or authorities; all things have been created through him and for him.

Colossians 1:9–16

# PART 1

## LIFE IS A JOURNEY

In the first part of this book, I want to give you a foundation for viewing life as a journey. I will also try to answer some of life's big questions: Where do we come from, and where are we going? You will also meet Jesus who is the ultimate source of all life.

# CHAPTER 1

## IS THERE A WAY FORWARD FOR HUMANITY?

"Evil has many faces, one of them is mine!"
/ Kjetil Hafstad

On any ordinary day, when we open the newspaper or scroll through the newsfeed on our mobile phones, it's easy to wonder where our world is heading. We can read about earthquakes, wars, and famines, and when I began writing this book, Covid-19 was sweeping across the globe, a pandemic that brought entire nations to a halt. Russia invaded Ukraine, and once again, there is war in Europe. Israel and the Middle East remain in constant media focus, with daily reports of terrorism, violence, and death. Suffering around the world is escalating, and the number of people fleeing war, starvation, and conflict has reached alarmingly high levels. In recent years, we have also faced increasingly extreme weather. Scientists warn that glaciers at both the North and South Poles are melting, causing sea levels to rise. Looking at the bigger picture, it feels as though the entire earth is groaning, and the world we live in is writhing in pain.

But, as we all know, we don't need to look at the global stage to see that the world is suffering. In the country where I live, Sweden, we read about shootings, gang-related crime, honor-based violence, abuse of power, and human trafficking. We witness how trust in our politicians and authorities is collapsing, and how the younger generation feels more and more discouraged as they lose hope for the future.

At the same time, it is easy to blame those in power for all the injustices that exists in the world, but it is rare that we see in our own lives those same seeds of evil. We are no longer living the lives that God from the beginning created us to live. Even though we have so much knowledge and understand the world better than ever before, we are unable to know and do what is right. We try to find our way by filling our lives with gadgets, experiences and relationships, hoping that they will give meaning to our lives. Freddie Mercury who was the lead singer of the rock group Queen said in one of his last interviews:

> "You can have everything in the world and still be the loneliest man. And that is the most bitter type of loneliness, success has brought me world idolization and millions of pounds. But it's prevented me from having the one thing we all need: A loving, ongoing relationship."

Though modern technology keeps us connected and ever within reach, a growing sense of loneliness continues to haunt many of us. Today we live in a time when everything goes faster, we fill our minds with impressions from social media and we can easily see what all our friends are doing. At the same time as life goes faster and faster, many ironically feel that life itself becomes more and more stagnant. We are not moving forward, and we are getting nowhere. We live for the moment and find no path that can take us further on. We dream of one thing after another in the hope that, that one thing, will take us to a better place in life where we don't feel so lonely and lost. But it doesn't take long for that feeling of emptiness to find us again. We keep adding to our already overcrowded lives, but we rarely subtract in order to make room for what truly matters. The actor and comedian Jim Carrey once said, "I think everybody should get rich and famous and do everything they ever dreamed of, so they can see that it's not the answer." I believe that deep down, we all know that the answer to our deepest longing cannot be found within ourselves or in any material riches this world has to offer.

The prophet Isaiah was spot on when he says "we all, like sheep, have gone astray, each of us has turned to our own way" (Isaiah 53:6). Jesus observed the same thing when he saw that people "were harassed and helpless, like sheep without a shepherd" (Matthew 9:36). But perhaps Paul best captures this inner brokenness of the soul whit his blunt confession that "I do not do the good I want to do, but the evil I do not want to do – this I keep on doing." (Romans 7:19). And I am willing to bet that we all, to some degree, recognize that his words apply to us all.

## Why do we exist?

Throughout the ages, humanity has wrestled with the questions. "Who are we?" and "Why do we exist?". This kind of questions are deeply rooted in every one of us and to know where we come from is a big part of understanding who we are. I heard the simplest explanation for why we humans exist from the English Bible teacher and pastor David Pawson. He said that "God had a son whom he loved so much that he wanted a bigger family, with more sons and more daughters."

Of course, we can never equate ourselves with God's only Son, but at the same time Paul said that God before the creation of the world has "predestined us for adoption to sonship through Jesus Christ" (Ephesians 1:4-5). God, who is complete and perfect in his communion between Father, Son and Spirit, wants us to be included in this divine fellowship ( John 17:21). When the disciple John writes his first letter, he states this mind-blowing truth that "God is love" (1 John 4:8). The Greek word for love is *agape* which has the meaning of an unconditional, outpouring selfless love. Even if we cannot fully comprehend the depth of the mystery of the Trinity, we are still invited to join in God's agape love. Unlike *eros,* which is erotic love and *phileo,* which describes the love between friends, agape is freely given and perfect in its unselfishness. When God created us, it was so that we can be included in His divine perfect love. God's intention has always been that we should be His sons and daughters (Ephesians 1:5). It is in this love that we are created to live, and we are to freely pass on this agape love just as we ourselves freely received it. God invites us to walk with Him, to reflect His love and glorify Him with our lives.

God in his greatness has chosen to draw near to us. A verse in the Bible that I find deeply touching can be found in Genesis chapter three, where we can read the beautifully description of how "They heard the sound of the Lord God as he was walking in the garden in the cool of the day" (Genesis 3:8). Just imagine what an amazing God we believe in, who doesn't want us to wander away from him but who longs for a close relationship with us. A walk where we can hear God's own footsteps while the cool evening wind blows through our hair.

This is why God placed the fragile gift of free will in man's hands and that is a great gift, an enormous trust, and at the same time an immense responsibility. Managing this free will can bring life and make life flourish, but the same time free will can also throw the world into death, darkness, and despair. The great theologian of the 13th century, Thomas Aquinas, recognized this and argued that good can exist without evil, but that evil cannot exist without goodness. As human beings, we stand in the midst of this tension between good and evil. In the first chapters of the Bible, it is the tree of knowledge of good and evil that becomes the symbol of this free will. Adam and Eve were faced with the free choice of either continuing to walk on God's good way or departing onto a path of their own, following the desires of their hearts. In the words of Paul, we were "gratifying the cravings of our flesh and following its desires and thoughts." (Ephesians 2:3)

DAY
3

## Where did we go wrong?

In Nicky Gumbel's classic book *Questions of Life*, there is a story about a British newspaper that announced a competition in which readers were asked to write an essay on the theme "What is wrong with the world?" Thousands of entries were submitted, but the winning response was also the shortest. It read: Regarding your article 'What's Wrong with the World? I am. Yours truly." It is said that the author G.K. Chesterton wrote this response, and in his book with the same title, *What's Wrong with the World*, he insightfully wrote: "It isn't that they can't see the solution. It is that they can't see the problem." Seeing ourselves as part of the world's problems is precisely what Paul is referring to when he writes that "all have sinned and fall short of the glory of God" (Romans 3:23). It may be tempting to think that God has failed in His creation, but in reality, it is creation that has failed to honor and glorify its Creator. God made us in His own image, with emotions and the capacity to love. But all true love originates from God's gift of free will, and therefore, love can never be forced. If God had created us without the ability to say no or to turn away from Him, there would be no true love. There might be respect, admiration, or fear, but not love. Love, by its very nature, must be rooted in the freedom to choose. We can only love if we are also free to reject love. This is what makes love incredibly beautiful, and at the same time, deeply vulnerable and fragile.

We know what choices Adam and Eve made, because that choice has haunted us ever since. As humanity, we have chosen the path of trying to find the answer to what is good and what is evil within ourselves. We listen to our hearts instead of listening to God's Word. But as Paul writes in the first chapter of his letter to the church in Rome, God has not abandoned His creation, for we can see "God's invisible qualities—His eternal power and divine nature—clearly seen in what has been made" (Romans 1:20). In his opening two chapters, Paul explains that God's law has been planted in us in the form of our conscience (Romans 1:18–32; 2:14–16). Therefore, people, including us, are without excuse (Romans 1:20). From God's point of view, He longs for us to return to a place where we once again learn to listen to His voice and allow Him to speak the truth we are meant to obey.

Everywhere evil is done, people get hurt, and it is always children and women who pay the highest price when abuses of power, oppression, war and violence are rampant. But if we are honest, we don't need to open up the newspapers to see how badly broken the world is, most of the time it's enough to just take a look in the mirror. So much of the world's hate, injustice, dishonesty and brokenness is right there in the reflection of our own lives. We don't even manage to live up to our own standards and our own ideals, we constantly struggle with bad habits and destructive behavior. Our ability to blame others has been sharpened into perfection throughout history, ever since that dark day when mankind walked away from God. On that day, Adam blamed Eve, and she in turn blamed the serpent. With frightening accuracy, we can see in ourselves the same unwillingness to take responsibility for our actions. It is this heritage from Eden, that makes us so reluctant to humble ourselves and come to God admitting that "I am" what is wrong with the world.

When the Bible talks about sin, this is what its writers are referring to. We no longer live the good lives that God created us to live. We have literally rebelled, missed the mark and gone astray and we are no longer walking through life in his presence. Therefore, sin is more a state of mind rather than some random wrong deeds that we occasionally do. My experience is that many people see sin, as doing actions that God has forbidden or doing things that God does not like, such as things that harm and hurt other people. Of course, sin can be all that since God didn't create us to hurt others. At the same time, sin is so much more than that, it is living our lives outside of God's perfect will and plan for our lives. Now you might be wondering "But doesn't that mean that everyone sins the whole time, since none of us are able to live perfectly and walk the way God wants us to?". Yes, that is exactly my point and what the Bible emphasizes.

Paul also makes this point when he in his letter to the church in Rome says, "for all have sinned and fall short of the glory of God" (Romans 3:23). It is all too easy to blame others for our bad behavior and make ourselves the victim. At times it seems like it's always someone else's fault. I have often heard people say that they "ended up in bad company", but I've rarely heard anyone admit they chose bad company. We see the faults in others much more easily than we see faults in ourselves. We say: "If only she... then I would!" Just imagine how many conflicts and broken relationships that could have been healed by a simple "I am sorry, it was all my fault."

Sometimes I have wondered what would had happened if, after the fall, Adam had said to God: "Don't blame Eve, It was me, I failed to take my responsibility, I'm sorry." We will probably never find the answer to that question, but just to think about it is exciting. The truth is that none, but you, can live your life. We all need to understand that we are responsible for the paths we choose to walk. Imagine if we all dared to admit that I am part of the world's problems and because of that, I am lost and in need of salvation. When I understand this fundamental truth, I can see myself in Paul's honest prayer: "What a wretched man I am! Who will rescue me from this body that is subject to death?" (Romans 7:24). After Paul wrote that "all have sinned and fall short of the glory of God" he then continues with the unthinkable truth that "all are justified freely by his grace through the redemption that came by Christ Jesus." (Romans 3:23-24). In other words, there is a way out of the grip that sin has held us in.

# Chapter 2

**THE CROSS IS THE CROSSROADS OF THE WORLD**

"The cross is the surest, truest and deepest window on the
very heart and character of the living and loving God."
/ NT Wright

Derek Redmond was born in 1965 and started his athletic career
at the age of seven. As a twenty-year-old, he broke the British
record for 400 meters. Unfortunately, his career was marked by
injuries and eleven times he was forced to have surgery done on
his knees and hamstrings. He was considered an extraordinary
talent who never got to show his full potential. In 1991, Tokyo
hosted the World Athletics Championships in track and field
and Derek was a part of the relay team that won the gold medal
as they defeated the heavily favored team from the USA.

The Barcelona Olympics in 1992 would be his grand finale,
where he finally would show the whole world his capabilities.
Since he was a child, his greatest desire had been to one day
stand as champion, with an Olympic gold medal around his
neck. Now he was one of the favorites. In Barcelona, Derek won
the qualifying race with the best time and when the gun went for
the semifinal, he was the big favorite. After he rounded the first
curve, about 175 meters into the race, he suddenly felt a pain in
his right leg. His hamstring had torn, and he fell face down to
the ground. Paramedics ran up to him to help him off the track,

but he fought them off. He stood up, and limping, made his way toward the finish line. The other runners reached the end of the track at the same time as Derek, who, in pain and agony, was fending off paramedics and officials while limping toward the finish. It started to get quiet in the stands. Then, a man in a cap and t-shirt ran up to Derek and said, "You don't have to do this." It was his father Jim, but Derek quickly replied: "I have to!". "Then we'll finish this together!" his father said, and they did. Derek's face was occasionally buried deep into his father's shoulder. While staying within his lane, they slowly approached the finish line. Applause then began to rise from the people in the stands and the cheers rose higher and higher. That day, Derek didn't walk away with a gold medal, but he did take with him a memory of his father, a father who could not stay in the stands as he saw his son suffer. He got up and passed through all the barriers to reach his son and help him finish the race.

The Gospel is the wonderful story of how God leaves the throne up in heaven and, in His love, He came down to help His children on earth find their way back home again. He is the one who created us, and He suffers when He sees us getting lost and when we hurting are stumbling along the path of life. Jesus said that this is why he has come, to "seek and save the lost" (Luke 19:10). Man's choice of path in the Garden of Eden led to sin entering into the world. We thought that if only we could decide for ourselves what way we should go, life would be better and greater. This turning away from God instead allowed the devil to gain a foothold in this world. That is why we in some of the letters of the New Testament can read things like "the whole world is under the control of the evil one." (1 John 5:19) and that "the creation is subjected to frustration" (Romans 8:20).

All throughout the Old Testament, we can follow the amazingly orchestrated story of how God calls out and chooses a people. A people through whom the Savior would come, the Messiah who one day was going to save the world. God himself had to become human just like us to be able to rescue us and atone for all our sin. This is something that the author of the book of Hebrews takes note of when he writes "Since the children have flesh and blood, he too shared in their humanity so that by his death he might break the power of him who holds the power of death - that is, the devil" (Hebrews 2:14). Therefore, it is impossible to understand or even talk about the Christian faith without talking about God becoming flesh and blood in the incarnation of Jesus. Jesus' life was a journey that led him to the cross, and on that tree of pain, God gave his life for us.

When our God left the throne room in heaven and entered into the world that he had created, he was born helpless in a stable. He grew up working as a carpenter in his father's company. Finally, at the age of 30, he stepped into the public light and introduced himself. In the midst of a fallen world, God himself now walked around in sandals and spoke about who God is and how much our heavenly Father wants us to find our way back home. He healed the sick and forgave sins, thereby showing that God is our physician, and that grace and forgiveness can only be found in Him. He is the light that entered our dark world and exposed the destructive powers of darkness. He cast out demons from the afflicted and by coming with light and freedom the confrontation with the dark principalities was inevitable ( John 3:19). The devil did not want to let go of the world he occupied and even though mankind could see the glorious light of Christ

Jesus, we chose darkness over light. The disciple John describes it with the words:

> Light has come into the world, but people loved darkness instead of light because their deeds were evil. Everyone who does evil hates the light, and will not come into the light for fear that their deeds will be exposed. ( John 3:19-20)

This turning away from God, is also described in the Old Testament by the prophet Isaiah who wrote: "We all, like sheep, have gone astray, each of us has turned to our own way; and the Lord has laid on him the iniquity of us all." (Isaiah 53:6). The Christian faith boils down to the unthinkable miracle that the creator of the whole universe chose to enter his own creation, leaving his heavenly stands to become like one of us. Jesus:

> Who, being in very nature God, did not consider equality with God something to be used to his own advantage; rather, he made himself nothing by taking the very nature of a servant, being made in human likeness. And being found in appearance as a man, he humbled himself by becoming obedient to death - even death on a cross! (Philippians 2:6-8).

Occasionally I am asked how an all-powerful and good God can create a system that ultimately requires him to sacrifice his own son in order to forgive our sins. If he is so great, awesome and good why can't he simply choose to forgive, just as you and I can choose to forgive? Well, the first mistake we make is that we try to understand God based on how we think as humans. There are, of course, several ingredients in this question, where everything ultimately boils down to who God actually is. We must begin with God, otherwise we will never realize the good news that we encounter in the gospel. Nor will we fully grasp why Jesus had to die such an agonizing death.

## God´s justice and love made visible

DAY 5

The apostle Paul wrote to the church in Rome that:

> "God presented Christ as a sacrifice of atonement, through the shedding of his blood – to be received by faith. He did this to demonstrate his righteousness, because in his forbearance he had left the sins committed beforehand unpunished, he did it to demonstrate his righteousness at the present time, so as to be just and the one who justifies those who have faith in Jesus." (Romans 3:25–26).

God who is by nature holy, loving and rich in grace and mercy is at the same time good, full of truth and justice. At a glance it may feel like an oxymoron. After all, aren't mercy and justice two opposite characteristics that tend to collide? Is it not through mercy that we can escape justice? But when we say that God is holy or set apart, we are not only describing what He is, at the same time we also describe what He is not. When we say that he is light, we also say that he is separated from darkness and therefore "in him there is no darkness at all." 1 John 1:5). Because God is truth, he is therefore separated from all lies. Since God is pure, there is no impurity to be found in him. He hates sin and what sin has done to His creation. But, if God is just, that must mean that God cannot forgive injustice, abuse or sin, for the simple reason that it cannot be reconciled with who

He is. God, who is completely just and holy, cannot allow murder, rape or lying to go unpunished. If he truly is just and righteous, he cannot simply forgive. God's justice demands that someone pays the price and takes the punishment for all the evil that mankind is guilty of. It includes the genocide in Nazi Germany, the murders in Rwanda, the abuse of children, the brutalities of ISIS, but also all the hate, indifference, lies, selfishness and greed that exist in our own lives. Paul drastically states the naked truth of our pitiful state when he says that "the wages of sin is death" (Romans 6:23).

When God became a man, like us, in Jesus, he was completely without sin. He made Himself to be the suffering servant as he was nailed to the cross. He became the sacrificial lamb who took upon himself the brutal punishment that justice demands. He who is good and just, punished sin and bore the judgment in his own body. At the cross he paid the wages of sin with his own death. Therefore, the death, burial and resurrection of Jesus are the most important events that have ever taken place in the history of the world. At the cross, justice was served and the penalty for all sin and evil has been fully paid forever. If you ever wonder what Gods view on rape, murder and pedophilia is, just take a look at the broken, tortured and bloody body of Jesus. God took upon Himself the price of our sins. The reason that we as humans can forgive abuse and injustice and show mercy is for the simple reason that we are neither perfectly good nor perfectly just. It is not fair to forgive a man who preyed on a weaker one, but it is merciful. This dilemma converges on the cross where we clearly can see God's justice and at the same time, his infinite grace and love.

At the cross, "God demonstrates his own love for us in this: While we were still sinners, Christ died for us" (Romans 5:8). It was out of his endless love that he chose to leave the throne of heaven to become a man ( John 3:16). We may think that God must have an inner conflict when He, on one hand cannot tolerate any kind of sin, in any form, but on the other hand He opens his arms to sinners. Maybe it sounds like a cliché, but in that case, it is a true cliché: God hates sin, but He loves sinners. Jesus never had a problem with people who confessed their wrongdoings, but he had continuous conflicts with the religious leaders who considered themselves to be pure, holy and sinless.

The gospel is not first and foremost God's solution to man's problem, but rather God's solution to his own problem. He had created a humanity that had turned its back on him. We wandered away from him and he longed to bring us back home. Just as in the parable of the prodigal son, we chose to leave our Heavenly Father and go our own way. But thanks to Jesus Christ, who is the way, the road to God is now open. We can leave the kingdom of darkness and step into the freedom of the kingdom of the Son he loves (Colossian 1:13). Some theologians speak of this as the "wonderful exchange" where I get to exchange my sin for His holiness and my death for His life. It is an amazing offer that Jesus gives us; we can go from being lost to being found, from being broken to being healed. God gives us this wonderful gift so that we can once again live our lives with the purpose and meaning that God wanted for us from the beginning of time. A life where none of the riches, adventures or pleasures of this world can ever compare to the grace, mercy and love that our righteous God in his great love gives us. We are now "created in Christ Jesus to do good works, which God prepared in advance for us to do." (Ephesians 2:10). If you want to know how far God was willing to go to welcome you into His family, just take a look at the cross of Calvary. It is easy to think that the cross was the end of Jesus' life, but in fact it was the beginning of what Jesus came to establish.

I am well aware that we cannot simply describe God's work on the cross as merely a penal substitution. The cross is so much more, it is a victory over the powers of evil, it is the price He paid to buy the world back to Himself and the ultimate proof of His grace and love. Theologian William H. Willimon describes it with the words "Jesus didn't die as a frustrated and failed revolutionary. His death was the revolution." It is in Christ's death we find forgiveness, and in his resurrection, we are raised to life in Him.

DAY 6

## Do you see the cross?

In the old hymn from 1912 by George Bennard we can sing:

> "On a hill far away stood an old rugged cross. The emblem of suffering and shame. And I love that old cross where the dearest and best for a world of lost sinners was slain."

It is a hymn that we often sang in the church that I grew up in as a child. This love for the cross of Jesus is a natural part of every Christian's life, or at least it should be. Looking to the cross, this instrument of torture, and making it to the ultimate symbol of love feels strange in a way. We hang the cruelest instrument of execution around our necks. The symbol of pain and shame has for many become the greatest proof of God's everlasting love and justice.

I still remember the day my grandmother told me about what had happened when my grandfather left this life to be with God. As a child, I spent quite a lot of time in Västerhaninge with my grandparents, Thure and Karin. This was during a period when my mother was ill after suffering from a severe goiter. I have many fond memories of my grandparents and was so sad when Grandpa passed away. Even though I was only six years old, I realized that I would never again take my grandfather's hand and walk into the forest with him. At a family gathering my grandmother talked to some of us younger grandchildren and told us about Thure's last days. He had suffered from severe cancer and spent his last days at home under my grandmother's care. Closer to his death, Thure could neither speak nor move. In response to questions, he could gently squeeze the hand and in that way communicate that he was still there. One day, Grandma heard a voice from Grandpa's room, and she thought she might had forgotten to turn off the radio. When she entered the room to her great surprise, she realized that it was Thure who was speaking. He said, "Do you see the cross?" All of a sudden, he sat up, raised his hand and pointed upwards, repeating: "Do you see the cross?" Grandma was there next to him when he once again said: "Do you see the cross? It is so wonderful". Then he lowered his arm and laid down on his pillow. Shortly afterwards he took his very last breath. When Grandma told us this, I was filled with a warm, vivid feeling that God really does exist, and that heaven awaits all who are God's children. Ever since then I have been absolutely sure of the reality of God. Even though I cherish that moment, I have come to understand that realizing God exists is not the same as making Jesus Christ my Lord.

The more I read the Bible and understand the magnitude of what Jesus did on the cross, the more I am filled with grandfather's words: "The cross, it's so wonderful." The cross of Jesus is wonderful because it opens a new way forward. Even if you have come to one of life's dead ends, God can change your course completely. The cross is the crossroad of the world and the turning point in human history and the empty tomb is the place that enables all of us to pass from eternal death to eternal life. At the first easter in 33 AD when Jesus died, was buried and rose from death, He forever changed the world. Paul writes in the opening praise of his letter to the Ephesians about the great mystery that God had planned since the dawn of time (Ephesians 1:3-14). On the cross, God summed up everything in heaven and on earth, the cross where Jesus gave his life is what everything points to. And one day when, like my grandfather, we close our eyes for the last time, it is the cross where Jesus gave his life that makes all the difference. Thanks to the cross, we are invited to finish our race with our heavenly Father. Thanks to the cross, death is defeated, and life lies ahead. (1 Corinthians 15:54-55).

# Chapter 3

## WE ARE ALL ON THE WAY

"Being a Christian is more than just an instantaneous
conversion – it is a daily process whereby
you grow to be more and more like Christ."
/ Billy Graham

While John Bunyan was in prison for preaching without the permission of the Church of England, he had a dream one night that later became his famous book *The Pilgrim's Progress*, first published in 1678. It describes Christian and his journey from his hometown "The city of Destruction" upon is soon to rain down fire and brimstone. With the burden of sin weighing heavily on his back, he sets out on a long journey where he faces many trials and hardships. At the Slough of Despond he almost drowns but is rescued by Help and climbs the hill of the cross where his burden falls from his shoulders. Later he is lured into Vanity Fair, where he is tempted to stay, thus ending his journey. Arriving at the Valley of the Shadow of Death, he is at first despondent but soon finds comfort and is able to move on. On the way, he also meets a number of different people. Faithful becomes his companion who proves to be a great support on his journey, but when Obstinate and the Giant Despair show up, they do everything they can to prevent Christian from reaching his goal, an eternal home in the Celestial City. The book was a success and for a couple of hundred years it was the most popular book in the world, second only to the Bible. Today it is no longer as well-known as it once was, but the story of life as a journey is still as relevant to us today as it was to the first readers of The Pilgrim's Progress.

When Paul writes his letter to the church in Ephesus, he repeatedly uses the language of the Way. Paul tells us to "Be very careful, then how you live, not as unwise but as wise" (Ephesians 5:15). The word *live* that Paul uses here is the Greek word *peripateō* which literally means "walk". According to Paul, we must be very careful how we "walk" our lives. If we are to see the Christian life as a journey, there are several questions that we need to ask ourselves: How does our journey begin? How do we get a good start? How do we faithfully continue our walk on the path? How do we avoid getting lost? And how can we manage to walk in a way that will bring us all the way home?

Paul frequently returns to the word *peripateō* to describe how we can walk through life. Another example of his use of the word can be found in the letter to the Colossians where he speaks of "living (walking) rooted and… strengthened in the faith" (Colossians 2:6-7). In total, Paul uses the word *peripateō* 31 times when he wants to convince us with the utmost clarity that we "walk" through life and that life is a journey. (A complete list of Bible words with the word *peripateō* can be found on page 169)

In his letter to the Ephesians, Paul says that we are created to "do the good works, which God prepared in advance for us to do." it is once again *peripateō* that he uses. We are to "walk in good works" (Ephesians 2:10). In this letter we are faced with two completely different ways in which we can walk through life. We can either walk "in transgressions and sins" (Ephesians 2:1-2), or we can walk in "good works" (Ephesians 2:10). Faced with this choice, it seems obvious that we should all choose to walk the path of good deeds rather than the path of sin. Unfortunately, however, that is not always the case. Furthermore, these two different ways of walking have radically different destinations. If we choose to walk in God's way, we are invited to a life where our walk with Him leads us to our final destination: His eternal kingdom, which Jesus will one day establish when He returns in glory.

It is no big surprise that Paul has picked up this road language of the way from his Jewish background, Pharisee as he was. When he uses the word *peripateō* it is with a clear connection to the Hebrew word *halacha* which literally means "the way". *Halacha* was the name that Jews had given to the part of the Talmud that contained the moral law. As a strict believing Jews Paul had to follow "the way" of the law to achieve righteousness.

When Paul then met Jesus and experienced God's boundless grace and love, it blew him away. He discovered that Jesus came to make those of us who believe in him, righteous before we even begin to walk with him. First God makes us righteous so that we, with the help of His Holy Spirit can walk a transformed life in righteousness. This life has grace as the engine and driving force. When Paul uses *peripateō* it is not to describe the way to salvation, but how we should walk our lives as forgiven and righteous. Our life with Jesus is a lifelong journey where we need his grace and wisdom in order to walk in all the good works which God prepared in advance for us to walk in.

The writer of Hebrews, whoever it was, is on the same track as Paul. Presumably he or she is speaking to a group of Christian Jews who, after Nero's deportation, were allowed to return to the city of Rome. They experienced a very difficult time, and it seems that they were considering leaving the path that they had started to walk on, despite having been enlightened and "tasted the goodness of the word of God and the powers of the coming age" (Hebrews 6:5). The Jews who received this letter were warned of leaving the way of salvation. The whole book of Hebrews is a therefore a long encouragement to be faithful and to keep walking on the way, without turning back.

At the same time, it is also a challenge for us today. As believers, we have all "come to share in Christ, if indeed we hold our original conviction firmly to the very end." (Hebrews 3:14). In this letter a fantastic picture is painted of Jesus as the one who fulfills all of the old covenant. We as readers are encouraged to let "this hope be an anchor for the soul" (Hebrews 6:19). To drive this point home the writer reminds us of several heroes of the faith whose examples we are to follow. These were people who walked by faith and steadfastly held on to Gods promises even though "none of them received what had been promised" (Hebrews 11:1-40). Through their wonderful example we as God's people are encouraged in a wonderful way to "throw off everything that hinders and the sin that so easily entangles. And let us run with perseverance the race marked out for us[...] so that we will not grow weary and lose heart." (Hebrews 12:1,3).

## The way to salvation!

When the New Testament talks about salvation it is the Greek word *sōzō* that is used. For all of us Bible geeks, it is interesting to dig down and look at the biblical grammar to see how the word is used. Sometimes there are nuances that we easily miss when the texts are translated into another language. The writers of the Bible use three different tenses when they talk about being saved: past, present and future. We therefore can read that we have been saved, that we are being saved and that one day we will be saved. An example of the past tense can be found in Paul's second letter to Timothy, where he writes that God *"has saved us* and called us to a holy life - not because of anything we have done but because of his own purpose and grace. This grace was given us in Christ Jesus before the beginning of time,"
(2 Timothy 1:9, my emphasis).

This is just one example of many, showing that salvation is placed at the start of the journey. It is described as something that already has happened, and the basis for it is Jesus' death on the cross. At the same time, Peter writes in his first letter how baptism has a parallel to the ark that saves Noah from the flood. He writes of a "baptism *that now saves you* also – not the removal of dirt from the body but the pledge of a clear conscience toward God. *It saves you* by the resurrection of Jesus Christ" (1 Peter 3:21, my emphasis). In other words, we can both look back on our salvation at the same time as we are now being saved. The third tense can be found in the letter to the Romans when Paul writes:

> "Since we have now been justified by his blood, how much more *shall we be saved* from God's wrath through

him! For if, while we were God's enemies, we were reconciled to him through the death of his Son, how much more, having been reconciled, *shall we be saved through his life!*" (Romans 5:9–10, my emphasis).

In other words, the Bible speaks of our salvation as something that has happened, something that is happening now, and something that is going to happen. When we compile all the different verses in the New Testament with the word *sōzō in,* an interesting and clear pattern emerges. In fact, most verses about salvation places it in the future as they speak of us becoming saved and that we one day can reach our salvation. This means that for all of us who believe in Jesus as our savior, salvation is past, present, and future at the same time. Salvation is not an event that we pass by on our journey but rather the very road we walk with our savior. We are walking on the road of salvation where somethings are left behind and something absolutely amazing is waiting ahead. It is only when we have persevered to the end of the road that we can reach the ultimate goal, "the salvation of our souls" (1 Peter 1:9).

## Jesus our savior!

Another way to look at our salvation is to see who Jesus is and what he came to do. The name Jesus comes from the Hebrew name "Yeshua" which means "God saves" and Jesus came to save us from our sins (Matthew 1:21). John the Baptist also understood this when he suddenly stopped, raised his arm, pointed at Jesus as he uttered the words: "Look, the Lamb of God, who takes away the sin of the world!" ( John 1:29). It is to save us from our sin that Jesus came to earth and that is also what the cross ultimately is about. But if that is true, then, then I am not completely saved yet because sin still affects me in so many ways. As we have previously discussed, it is sin that is our greatest enemy. In the atonement, Jesus saves us from sin on three different levels. Through Jesus' death we are saved from the *penalty* of sin (1 Pet 2:24) and we can walk in the assurance that we are forgiven and now belong to the kingdom of God. Atonement also enables us to overcome sin in our own lives as sin more and more loses its power over us. We can therefore, with God's help, be saved from the *influence* of sin as we are being transformed and changed by Jesus (Romans 6:1-14). But the cross also gives us the certainty that we will one day be completely free even from the very *presence* of sin when we are united with him in the coming glory (Revelations 21:3–4).

To make it a little easier, we can use three classic theological expressions that can help us to better understand how Jesus saves us from our sin. These three words are *justification*, *sanctification*, and *glorification*, three words that are often found in the Bible. These three words also corresponds with both the three tenses that we talked about earlier as well as how Jesus saves us from sin.

- *First*: as Christians, we are *justified* (past tense) and freed from the penalty of sin. This happens as we make Jesus our Lord and Savior and we become born again.
- *Secondly*: right now, we are *sanctified* (present) as we become increasingly transformed and freed from the influence of sin. This happens step by step when we, learn

to be with Jesus and with God's help, resist the devil and the temptation to sin.

- *Thirdly*: one day (future tense) we will be *glorified* when we are united with Him and are forever freed from the presence of sin.

When the Bible talks about our salvation, these three words often appear together: our past justification, our on-going sanctification, and our future glorification. Therefore, salvation is not a stop that we pass by on the road to heaven, but rather the very road on which we travel. It is in this same manner that the writers of the Bible describes salvation. This is also why we "continue to work out (our) salvation with fear and trembling" (Philippians 2:12). "Christ was sacrificed once to take away the sins of many; and he will appear a second time, not to bear sin, but to bring salvation to those who are waiting for him." (Hebrews 9:28).

Perhaps this is a completely new way of thinking for you. Maybe you find the way you normally think about your faith is being turned upside down. If so, I would like you to consider changing the way you think about your salvation, and I hope that this new way of thinking gives you an even greater and bigger picture of how Jesus wants you to walk. The salvation that Jesus came to give us has happened, is happening, and will be completed when Jesus returns and establishes His kingdom here on earth. Therefore, it is not possible to place God's *sōzō* at any single point on the journey so that we can say, "I was saved a long time ago" for the simple reason that we have not yet fully received all of God's salvation. However, if we walk with Christ and let his Spirit lead us, we are well on our way to being saved.

## Back to the language of the road

The language of the road helps us to get a better and a more correct view of the Christian life. We are called to embark on a journey together with Jesus. When Jesus called his disciples, it was with the classic words "Come, follow me!" (Mark 1:17). Jesus said of himself that he is "the way, the truth, and the life" ( John 14:6), and he spoke of our need to walk on "the narrow path that leads to life" (Matthew 7:13-14). Perhaps it is therefore not so surprising that the first words used to describe the Christians were words like "followers" (Ephesians 5:1), "disciples" (Acts 6:7) or simply just those "who belonged to the Way" (Acts 9:2). The Bible thus uses "the Way" both to describe Jesus as the way to salvation and the way in which we are to live out our faith in him.

If salvation is reduced to only referring to a specific day and hour then we risk giving new believers a bad start. When Jesus called his disciples, it was to walk with him. When he said, "Come, follow me!" their "Yes" was of utmost importance but without their continued following their initial "Yes" would soon have lost all of its meaning. God calls us to embark on a journey where we, like Paul, can say that we are "Forgetting what is behind and straining toward what is ahead, I press on toward the goal to win the prize for which God has called me heavenward in Christ Jesus." (Philippians 3:13–14). In other words, there is a clear goal for us to walk towards and we are mistaken if we think we have already "obtained all this, or have already arrived at our goal, but we press on to take hold of that for which Christ Jesus took hold of us." (Philippians 3:12). It is also for that reason that we are urged to "keep in step with the Spirit"

(Galatians 5:25) and that we must not leave "the straight way and wander off." (2 Peter 2:15). As I hope you now notice, the writers of the Bible uses this language of "walking" in their way of talking about the Christian life. When Jesus' younger brother James ends his short letter, he appeals to its readers to help those who have departed from God's way. He says that "Whoever turns a sinner from the error of their way will save them from death and cover over a multitude of sins." ( James 5:20). As followers of Jesus, we are called to walk in His footsteps and follow the paths that God invites us all to take. As disciples, we are clearly on a journey and the path we are on has a clear goal. Hopefully you will continue this journey until the day on which you will be "receiving the end result of your faith, the salvation of your souls." (1 Peter 1:9). Then our journey is over, and the heavenly party can begin. On that day I can boldly and loudly proclaim: "I am now saved!" and that "I have finally received the full salvation that Jesus died for!"

# PART 2

## A GOOD START

In the second part of the book, we will encounter the teachings of the early church and take a closer look at what they considered the first and most important steps of the journey.

In order to walk steadily, persistently, and with strength, we need to get a good start on our journey as we travel on the road to salvation.

# Chapter 4

## THE IMPORTANCE OF A GOOD START

"So then, just as you received Christ Jesus as Lord, continue to
live (walk) your lives in him, rooted and built up in him,
strengthened in the faith as you were taught,
and overflowing with thankfulness."
Colossians 2:6–7

I'm not a fanatic when it comes to sports, but when it's time for
the Olympics or the World Cup, my interest is usually
awakened. Watching the 100 meters final of the Olympics is
always just as exciting. There are often one or two clear
favorites, but no matter how fast they run, everything can be lost
because of a bad start. The margins in a race are so small that a
delay of a fraction of a second at the start can make the
difference between winning or losing. In a similar way, when
you build a house, it doesn't matter how beautiful and stylish
the structure above ground is if the foundation hasn't been laid
properly. Equally important is getting a good start on our
Christian walk, as this forms the foundation that will make all
the difference.

During my years as a pastor, I have seen many amazing proofs
of God's ability to transform people's lives. The cross is truly
"the power of God that brings salvation to everyone who
believes" (Romans 1:16). God shows again and again, his

willingness to transform and restore even the most lost and broken people. I have seen children, young adults, and elderly people come to know Jesus. I have attended Alpha and observed how people without any previous knowledge of God have found a personal relationship with a living God. Being able to listen when someone is formulating their own prayer for the first time is one of the best things I know. At other time I have seen with sadness how Christians have struggled to hold on to their faith in God. Every time I see a person leave our Lord and savior and walk away from their faith, something in my heart breaks. That pain is so great.

As a pastor, I have had many opportunities to talk to young people about life and faith. One advantage of being a pastor for almost 17 years in one and the same congregation was that I got to follow many people from birth to baptism and from youth into adulthood. Many times, I also had the opportunity to reflect on what causes some to walk astray while others seem to walk in faith with ever firmer and steadier steps. The question of a good start has really troubled me, and through the years I pondered over several different explanations. Many who grow up in church have been formed in an environment where it is mandatory to believe in the existence of God. In addition, their friends share the same worldview, and they learn about God and develop an understanding of right and wrong. They hear testimonies of divine interventions, of people being healed and of other miracles. Their belief in the existence of God is strengthened and they begin to live their lives with a Christian lifestyle. Often, they succeed quite well and probably they think that they are rather good people since they neither swear nor smoke. To borrow an expression that I heard from my friend

Hans Jansson, "many have to a large extent been socialized into the Christian faith". For some, that can be a good thing, as it may enable them to embrace many good values that could save them from making a lot of foolish mistakes. For others, however, this socialization into the Christian faith may go no further than a belief in God's existence. They may have simply reduced the Christian life to doing the right things or adhering to the right beliefs and values.

If we only have been socialized into the Christian faith, we are not living with Jesus as our Lord. Rather we are living on our own terms but in hope that God will be there for us when we need him. I realize that it is still possible for those who think of God in this way to find Jesus along the way, when they realize that our faith is not just a belief in His existence, but rather about getting to know Him as our Lord.

The message we encounter when we open the Bible is, in many ways, both disturbing and challenging. We realize that it is not possible to gradually grow into God's family simply by believing the right things. It is only when we, in faith, acknowledge Jesus as our Lord and Savior that we die to our old life and rise to a new life together with Him. This new life in Christ is what makes it possible for us to enter into a personal relationship with God as our Father. In other words, you cannot be very Christian or just a little bit Christian. You are either a child of God, with Jesus as your Lord, or you are not. The gospel, which means "the good news," can only become good news when we realize and accept that there is also bad news. The bad news is that we all "were dead in our trespasses and sins" (Ephesians 2:1) and that "all have sinned and fall short of the glory of God" (Romans 3:23). As Christians, we need to understand the serious nature of what we are part of, real people risk being lost for eternity if they don't know Jesus as Lord and Savior. There are many roads we can take in life, but there is only one road that leads to God ( John 14:6). That's why, as His church, we need to talk about the necessity of making Jesus the Lord and Master of our lives, and not be satisfied when someone merely expresses a belief in God's existence. Faith in Jesus is a lifelong journey, not just a one-way ticket to heaven. We need to actively help everyone who begins to believe in Jesus to get the best possible start on their journey, regardless of age or background. As a church, we carry a great responsibility to guide people to the right path, so they don't get lost along the way. The truly good news is that we are not alone in this. God Himself is building His church in this world through His Holy Spirit.

To be completely honest, I must admit that I too, to some extent, has been socialized into the Christian faith. Don't get me wrong, I'm incredibly grateful for everything I received from my family and church while growing up, but on its own, that is not enough. The faith planted in our lives must lead to a personal decision to declare Jesus as Lord and Savior. I clearly remember the day when, for the first time, I became aware of my sin and felt the heavy burden of sorrow fall upon me. It happened while I was with my family at my grandparents' old farm somewhere between Skövde and Falköping. It was a small croft without electricity or running water. We fetched water from a well using a manual pump, and when night came, we lit a fire and used candles for light. One night, I couldn't sleep as a deep sense of worry and sorrow slowly came over me. All of a sudden, I realized that I actually didn't know Jesus, even though I had grown up in a Christian home and gone to church every Sunday. With a mix of sadness and fear, I called out to my father. He came into my room, sat down by the bed, and asked me what was wrong. Then, after a short father-to-son conversation, he led me in a simple prayer where I asked for forgiveness for my sins. Even though I was very young, I still look back on that moment as the point at which I was saved. Today, I would say that it was then and there my journey with Jesus began, and when I first recognized my need for forgiveness. Since then, I've felt the need to ask for forgiveness more times than I can count. I received a deep longing to know Him more, to discover His way, and to follow Jesus wherever He leads. At the time, I was just a young boy, but a few years later, at the age of ten, I was baptized and became involved in the church my family attended. However, it wasn't until my teenage years that faith truly took hold of me and Jesus became real to me. It was also during those years that I had my first real encounter with the Holy Spirit. It was like a switch flipped inside me. God became real to me, He started to work inside of me as I began reading the Bible and making prayer a natural part of everyday life. Now I was on God's Road, and since then, I have never left "God's path", but I must be honest and say that I haven't always kept in step with Jesus. Like everyone else, I've faced struggles and have often had to remind myself of what truly matters, and what kind of life I want to live. Like so many others, I long to seek God, yet I've often wrestled with the question of how to do that, and how to make space for the Holy Spirit to lead me. As a slow reader, I've found it challenging to read the Bible, and it hasn't always been easy to understand how God's Word can guide me in my everyday walk with Him.

Sadly, I must admit that, as a church, we have often failed by socializing young people and new believers into the faith without giving them the best possible start on their journey with God. Personally, as I mentioned earlier, I am ever grateful to my parents, the leaders at my church and to my friends for what they did for me during my upbringing. However, I can see that sometimes we have thrown people out on a journey of faith without walking with them as they take their first steps with Jesus.

When I read about the first disciples in the Acts of the Apostles, it sometimes feels as they lived the Christian life differently than we do today, at least us here in Sweden. It seems like they all were totally absorbed by Jesus and that nothing could stop them from living out their faith, no matter the circumstances. They had a boldness and a passion to tell other people about the risen living Jesus, even though they experienced tribulation, persecution, contempt and were thrown into prison. Sometimes I wonder why there is such a difference between their faith and ours. Could one reason be that they didn't "inherit" their faith in the way that many Christians in the West have done? But after meeting people from many different parts of the world I have come to realize that wherever you are from, socialization into the Christian faith is to be found everywhere. So, in the end it all boils down to one thing: do we know Jesus personally as our Savior or do we just know about him. Sound theology, appropriate behavior and good moral standards are important, but what we need most is a living ongoing relationship with our God and Father. The kind of relationship where He so fills our lives that "we cannot help speaking about what we have seen and heard." (Acts 4:20).

## A good start

On the day of Pentecost there was an explosive growth of new believers, and that was just on the very first day of the early church. "Those who accepted his message were baptized, and about three thousand were added to their number that day." (Acts 2:41). As we read further in the book of Acts, we discover how the early church made sure that new pilgrims on the path of faith received the best possible start. It is in this book; Luke gives us the clearest picture of what the early church emphasized as they helped people follow Jesus. The pattern that emerges is of a church that guided new believers through four distinct steps, steps that gave them a solid foundation for their walk of faith. Peter preached on the day of Pentecost about Jesus as the Messiah, and "When the people heard this, they were cut to the heart and said to Peter and the other apostles, 'Brothers, what shall we do?'" (Acts 2:37). What we read next reveals what the apostles saw as the foundation and starting point of our journey with Jesus.

On the day of Pentecost, Peter spoke to Jews who already believed in God's existence. Now they heard about Jesus and believed that He was their long-awaited Messiah. Peter raised his voice and told the people, "Repent and be baptized, every one of you, in the name of Jesus Christ" (Acts 2:38). When we repent, believe, and are baptized, we are cleansed and forgiven, and we receive the forgiveness of our sins. But God does not leave new believers there, clean and forgiven. He also promises to fill them with His very presence as they "receive the gift of the Holy Spirit" (Acts 2:38). This became the template and the way the first Christians used to guide new believers on their journey.

Without these first basic steps, we will most certainly limp through life and struggle in our faith. Limping can tire out even the most persistent traveler and cause them to give up when their strength runs out. I feel somewhat embarrassed to admit that I, as a pastor, have only now truly discovered the four steps, but that's not entirely the case. Repentance, faith, baptism, and life in the Spirit have always been a part of my faith journey, but they are things I have occasionally taken for granted, without recognizing their full significance in my everyday walk with Jesus. It was when I listened to the British Bible teacher David Pawson that I really began to understand the importance of these steps, and it slowly began to take root in my heart. When he pointed out these foundational steps, I had to stop and pause the recording. For a couple of days, I listened to it again and again, and I started to search God's Word, as I now began to see things I hadn't previously seen with such clarity. This awakened something within me, a hope to better help people on their walk with Jesus. The first steps the apostles led people through were repentance, faith in God, baptism in water, and receiving the Holy Spirit. There is a risk that we nod in recognition without ever truly grasping the importance of these steps. They are central and decisive for a person's entire relationship with Jesus. Yet, I have met many in our churches who are missing one or more of these foundational steps in their walk with Him.

When Paul later came to the city of Ephesus on his journey through Asia Minor, we read in Acts 19 that he met some disciples and asked them about the beginning of their faith journey. "Did you receive the Holy Spirit when you believed?"

he asked. They answered, "No, we have not even heard that there is a Holy Spirit" (Acts 19:1–2). Reading further, we see that this response made Paul curious, so he asked, "Then what baptism did you receive?" "John's baptism," they replied (Acts 19:3). From their answer, Paul gained a clearer picture of their situation. They had not yet received the Christian baptism into Christ, but only John's baptism of repentance. This needed to be corrected. Paul explained that John "told the people to believe in the one coming after him, that is, in Jesus" (Acts 19:4). When the disciples in Ephesus heard this message of repentance and faith, they were baptized in the name of the Lord Jesus. Paul then laid his hands on them, and the Holy Spirit came upon them. They spoke in tongues and prophesied. Now, they could truly begin their journey on the path of salvation, converted, cleansed, and filled with God's presence (Acts 19:1–6).

When the writer of Hebrews talks about "the elementary teachings about Christ", it is these steps that he refers to (Hebrews 6:1–2). We all need these steps in our lives. The problem is that those who received this letter did not have all the pieces in place. The author writes that they should, by now, be teaching others but instead they once again need someone to teach them the basics of God's Word. First he mentions "repentance from acts that lead to death." (Hebrews 6:1) This is also what Jesus spoke of at the beginning of his earthly ministry: "The time has come, he said. The kingdom of God has come near. Repent and believe the good news!" (Mark 1:15). The second thing the author of the book of Hebrews mentions is "faith in God" where we learn to trust in God and in his word for guidance. Then he mentions "instructions about cleansing rites and the laying on of hands" (Hebrews 6:1-2). Cleansing rites or baptism is indeed a clear visible marking in the Christian faith, but baptism is so much more than just an act of symbolism. The fact that the author then talks abouts the laying of hands instead of being filled with the Holy Spirit is probably for the simple reason that in most cases it was through the laying on of hands that the Holy Spirit was received in the New Testament.

The last two foundations mentioned here in Hebrews are the resurrection of the dead and eternal judgment. Both concern the end of the journey rather than its beginning. Nevertheless, teaching about the resurrection of the dead and the return of Jesus were common themes in the early church and were considered as elementary teachings. We must never lose sight of the fact that Jesus will one day return in glory to judge the living and the dead (2 Tim 4:1). After reminding the readers of these foundations of faith, the author expresses his own longing and hope that they, God permitting, will press on forward (Hebrews 6:3). But that can only happen after the foundation is put in place. In the next four chapters, we will delve deeper into these first steps of our walk: repentance, faith, baptism, and receiving the Holy Spirit. It is my longing that together we can build a solid foundation for a strong beginning, one that will make our journey with Jesus firmer and stronger, to the glory of God.

# Chapter 5

## THE JOURNEY BEGINS WITH REPENTANCE

"The forgiveness of sins through repentance shall
be proclaimed in his name to all nations."
Luke 24:47

When Jesus first began his ministry at the age of 30, he had a clear message of repentance. He proclaimed the good news of the kingdom and challenged all to turn around and change their way of living (Matthew 4:17). He spoke of the importance of making a spiritual U-turn and charting a new course in life, marked by a new way of thinking. When Jesus emphasized the need for repentance it was like a coin with two sides. On the one side we need to turn our backs on our sin, but on the other side we need to turn our lives and faces towards God.

Both for Jesus and for the first Christians, repentance was an integral part of their teaching. When Jesus later summed up his ministry, he said that "The Messiah will suffer and rise from the dead on the third day, ant repentance for the forgiveness of sins will be preached in his name to all nations, beginning at Jerusalem" (Luke 24:47). After the people had heard Peter preach on the day of Pentecost, they asked him and the other disciples, "Brothers, what shall we do?" Peter began his answer with the word: "Repent" (Acts 2:38). Repentance is the natural consequence when God starts to work in our lives, and we are faced with the gospel of Jesus Christ. It was the preaching of the Word that caused Peter's listeners to take the vital first step of repentance. God's word is living and active, it shows us what we are really like and points to our need of a savior. Repentance is the start of the journey of faith and a prerequisite for the work of salvation to begin in our lives. It is this attitude that we need to adopt as we become children of God. Repentance tears down our walls of pride and pulls up our roots of self-righteousness. Repentance changes our direction in life so that our goal becomes walking in fellowship with Christ with our faces turned towards God.

However, no one's journey is the same as anyone else's. Sometimes a person's journey toward God begins with an inner conviction of His existence and a realization that He is real. This is what Paul refers to in his letter to the Romans when he writes, "Since the creation of the world God's invisible qualities, His eternal power and divine nature—have been clearly seen, being understood from what has been made" (Romans 1:20). Some people simply begin to realize that there must be a Creator behind creation. This belief leads them to explore what the Christian faith is all about. I have also met people who grew up in the church and became convinced of God's existence when they heard about Him or witnessed wonders and miracles performed by His hand. Others begin their journey when they are confronted with God's Word, as Peter's listeners were on the day of Pentecost (Acts 2:37). They understood that Jesus was indeed their long-awaited Messiah. This first conviction can be experienced by some as a deep sorrow when they realize they haven't lived as they should and have broken divine law. Others develop an inner longing for something more in life, which leads them to start searching for its meaning. When we turn to God and invite Him into our lives, it sparks a renewal of our minds, and bit by bit, we begin to include God in our way of looking at the world. Another common way to begin a journey toward God is through a time of crisis or grief. In these situations, a word or event can bring us to a point where, in desperation, we surrender to God and acknowledge our need for Him. However, this surrendering of ourselves to God in repentance is crucial for everyone who wants to walk the path of salvation, whether they grew up in church or realized later in life that God is the Creator and Lord.

Repentance is the first step where we make the U-turn required to be able to leave the old road behind and start walking on the new road that Jesus has opened up for us. But we must never forget that salvation is not based on our own efforts, but rather it is a part of a greater transaction. God is there when we repent and when we draw near to Him, He draws near to us ( James 4:8). The only reason that we can love God at all is because He first loved us (1 John 4:19). Faith begins to shape in me as I look up to the only one who can save me. In Psalm 121 the psalmist exclaims: "I lift up my eyes to the mountains: where does my help come from?" Then he answers his own rhetorical question with the words "My help comes from the Lord, the maker of heaven and earth." (Psalm 121:1–2). That is where conversion begins.

I said that one side of the coin of repentance is to *turn away* from what the Bible calls sin. Today, sin is a more or less a word that has been eliminated from our vocabulary and many times it feels foreign and judgmental to even put that word in one's mouth. Talk of sin usually leads to one of two reactions: defense or attack. The defenders claim that they are certainly not all that bad, but are rather quite good, at least in comparison to others. After all, there are many who are a much worse a sinner than I am. The attacker, on the other hand, says that we shouldn't stick our nose into other people's business and judge their lifestyles. Maybe they point the finger back at us saying "And who are you to judge me?" Opening the Bible in circumstances such as these can lead to a clash with our way of thinking. In fact, the Bible answers the question of sin in an entirely different way namely the way of confession. We should neither become defensive nor go on the attack, but instead we should just be honest about our sin and confess that: I have sinned. It is a blessing and a relief to come before God and confess one's sins and then to be met with grace, mercy, love and forgiveness ( John 1:9, James 5:16).

**DAY 12**

## That thing with sin...

On 30 November 1916 the streets of Vienna were filled by people in mourning. Emperor Franz Josef I was to be buried that day. After 68 years on the throne, he was mourned by many and had left a powerful imprint on the political scene in Europe. As the cortege made its way through the streets of Vienna it approached the Capuchin Crypt. When they arrived at the burial place they were met by a closed iron gate. The archduke at the head of the procession knocked on the gate and shouted: "Open!".

"Who are you? Who asks to enter?" asked a cardinal from the other side of the iron gate. The archduke answered: "We carry with us the remains of the emperor, the apostolic royalty Franz

Joseph I, by the grace of God Emperor of Austria, King of Hungary, Defender of the True Faith." The archduke then proceeded to read all of the 37 titles that Franz Josef bore at the time of his death. When he has finished a hush fell over the place. The voice was once more heard from the other side of the massive gate to the crypt, "We know him not!". Again, the archduke knocked, and the procedure was repeated, but once again the voice replied, "We know him not!". When the third knocking had faded out the cardinal asked once more: "Who asks to enter?". In a somewhat subdued voice, the archduke replied: "We carry with us the body of Franz Joseph, our brother, a sinner like us all." After these words the great iron gates swung open and the Emperor of Austria could be carried to his final resting place.

We are all sinners, and we need to release that. When we come to Jesus, who is the light of the world, our sin and our filth is brought out into his light and made visible. For many of us, it can be an uncomfortable, revealing, and painful process. No titles or achievements can hide the fact that sin is there deep inside our hearts. Confession of this sin opens the door to a life of forgiveness and fellowship with God.

After a long and hard day on the lake, Jesus stepped into Simon Peter's boat. Jesus, himself a carpenter by trade, told the fisherman Peter to throw his nets back out on the other side of the boat. Somewhat reluctantly, Simon Peter did as Jesus said and soon his nets were filled to the brim with fish. Peter suddenly realized who had stepped into his boat and shouted: "Go away from me, Lord; I am a sinful man!" (Luke 5:8). What Jesus then chose to do may have shocked some, but it is completely in character with how God really is. Jesus invited this confessing sinner to come and follow him (Luke 5:10-11). Confessing sin is central to our relationship with God and has always been an important part of the Christian faith. Contrary to Franz Joseph, this confession needs to come from our own lips while we are still alive. However, sin can not only be described as disbelief in God. Sin can also be described as all the different things that we do that ultimately hurt our heavenly Father. As believers, we are called to turn away from our sins and leave them behind us so that we can receive forgiveness in order that God can purify us and dome to dwell in us by His Holy Spirit. This does not mean that we will never sin again. But when we turn to God, we take the first step on the road of salvation where we can find mercy and forgiveness for our sin.

Paul expresses the destructive power of sin with the words "you were dead in your transgressions and sins, in which you used to live (*walk*) when you followed the ways of this world." (Ephesians 2:1, italics mine). Our transgressions and sins lead to eternal death, and none of us can escape it, for all have sinned. Lying, slander, greed, hate, envy, having sex outside marriage; these are just a few of the actions and attitudes that hurts God because they go against what He created us for. Even our best and most noble deeds are often marked by ulterior motives, for example by our need of confirmation, or perhaps by pride or arrogance. Further on in his letter to the Ephesians, Paul reminds the church of the good news when he writes that "God, who is rich in mercy, made us alive with Christ even when we were dead in transgressions, it is by the grace you have been saved." (Ephesians 2 :4–5). This is God's beautiful grace, that despite our sin He loves us so deeply! God wants us to repent, not that He will be pleased, but for our sake. God wants us to live the life that He created us to live. Therefore, when the Bible talks about repentance, it is always with three different dimensions in mind: our thoughts, our words and finally our deeds.

## Repentance in thought

DAY
13

> "Do not be conformed to this world, but be transformed by the renewing of your thoughts so that you can determine what is the will of the Lord, what is good, perfect and pleasing to him." (Romans 12:2)

Letting one's thoughts be renewed is literally what repentance means. Although repentance first takes place at the start of our journey, we will never be able to leave it behind. Every day we need to repent, turn our face towards God and pray for a renewed mind. The Greek word for repentance is *metanoeō* which literally means "thoughts new" or "to think in a new way." God wants to change our thoughts and make us think in a new way about Him, ourselves and the world in which we live. For many of us, God's way of thinking is a challenge that often collides with the thoughts that we meet in the world around us. In a way, it has always been like this. When the New Testament was written, its writers lived in a culture where women and children were considered inferior. A woman in Greek culture was thought of as only half-human. The Greeks saw humility as a weakness that needed to be overcome, and generosity was a sign of a weak character. Today we can see in our culture just how much God's way of thinking has come to characterize western society in more ways than we think. Even if we see degradation of biblical morals, we still celebrate servant leadership, generosity, humility and the equality of all people. This is a result of the renewed mind that Christian faith has produced, and this has had a tremendous influence on our society.

New thoughts of repentance make us realize that it is God who is the center of everything and that we have dishonored Him in our thoughts, deeds and lives. This insight makes us agree with the words of the prodigal son who said: "I have sinned against heaven and against you" (Luke 15:18). Repentance leads us to the understanding that it is God's character that we have ultimately hurt, that we have failed to live the life that we were created to live and that we are in desperate need of His grace. In other words, God is kinder, purer and more just than I can comprehend, while I am more broken and sinful than I realize. People who do not believe in God often think the other way around; they like to tell God how He should behave in order for Him to be considered good and fair.

In his book *The Water Babies*, Charles Kingsley writes about Tom the sweeper boy who climbed up and down London's chimneys. Tom was dirty from all the soot and lived together with the other chimney boys. All of them were constantly dirty and because of that none of them saw it as a problem. In their own eyes, they were perfectly normal and as clean as boys should be. One day, when Tom was going to sweep a chimney, he entered a room where a girl was sleeping. They were in the same age and the girl was lying on a bed with white sheets and Tom thought that her skin was as white as snow. Ellie, as the girl was called, looked like an angel in Tom's eyes. Then he looked down at his own hands and clothes. Standing there next to her bed he suddenly realized how dirty and unclean he was. He wondered if he ever would be able to be as clean as Ellie.

This feeling of impurity became the starting point where his life began to change. The story of Tom is a great illustration of how blind we can be to our own sin and dirt, as long as we do not expose ourselves to that which is pure and holy. If we only compare ourselves with each other than we often feel alright, but when we look at Jesus, who is pure, holy, righteous and perfectly clean, we are made acutely aware of the dirt and sin that we carry in our own lives. The more we look at Jesus, the more we see our need of forgiveness and cleansing. Fixing our eyes on Jesus awakens a longing in us to do away with the sin that makes us dirty and to let God's forgiveness and life renew us so that we instead begin to see ourselves through God's loving eyes.

When Paul, in the twelfth chapter of Romans, urges us to "be transformed by the renewing of your mind," he simultaneously warns us "not to conform to the pattern of this world" (Romans 12:2). Either we are transformed, gaining more of God's thoughts through repentance and renewal, or we adopt the world's way of thinking by conforming to it. If we, as God's children, are to test and approve what God's will is (Romans 12:2b), that is, to understand what He wants us to do, we must make deliberate choices to let Him change the way we think. Yet even those of us who have begun this journey of letting God renew our minds may at times find ourselves drawn back into the world's way of thinking, again and again.

The word Paul uses for the transformation of our way of thinking is *metamorphoō*, the same word that we use to describe the metamorphosis a caterpillar undergoes as it turns into a butterfly. God sees a fantastic and beautiful butterfly in us, his "caterpillars", and He wants to leads us into the freedom that only transformation done by Him can bring. When God performs His metamorphosis in our lives, we can start to understand His will. Today, it is sadly more difficult than ever to avoid conforming to this world. Social media, movies, films, drama series, books and magazines preach worldly values right into our living rooms. We need to make active choices to reduce the voices of the world and their influence in our lives. Speaking personally, during certain periods in my life I have experienced God urging me to refrain from certain types of music or from watching certain films. Even if these were only small steps in the right direction, they still did wonders for my faith in God.

However, saying no to some voices is only one side of the equation. We also need to make conscious choices to follow the path where the Bible, prayer and the community of believers gets more space in our lives. It's amazing how even small steps can make a huge difference. God can, through His word and His Spirit start this amazing metamorphosis that we so much long for. We can go from being broken, sinful "caterpillars" to living holier and purer lives where we daily can allow God's new thoughts to help us determine what His will is. His great metamorphosis in us will lead us to the point where we are able to test and decern "what God's will is – His good, pleasing and perfect will." (Romans 12:3).

DAY
14

## Repentance in words

"If we claim to be without sin, we deceive ourselves and the truth is not in us. If we confess our sins, he is faithful and just and will forgive us our sins and purify us from all unrighteousness." (1 John 1:8–9)

If the first part of repentance take place in our thoughts, then the natural consequence of that is that we allow the repentance to manifest in our words. It is remarkable how much the Bible talks about using our mouths to express what is within us. Jesus clearly addresses this when he says the classic words: "For the mouth speaks what the heart is full of" (Luke 6:45b). What comes out of our mouths therefore reveals what is in our hearts. But God is not in the least afraid of what is inside of us. It may feel terrifying to openly speak about and put words to the darkest areas of our lives, but God loves that honesty and besides, we can't keep anything secret from God who already knows everything about us.

My own experience is that most Christians rarely have a problem confessing sin in general terms. We can say things like: "Of course I have sinned, who hasn't?" But it is rare that we stop and think about what sins we have committed and then start naming them by saying: "Father, forgive me for my greed/lies/envy/hatred/lust/apathy." Both God and you know the sins that dwells within you. As long as they are namelessly hidden, they can hold on to and exert their influence over us. As part of our repentance, we need to name our sins and call them out into the light. Our words matter and they affect our lives in more ways than we think, but our words also have an effect in the spiritual realm, and they can echo into eternity. There is an incredible power, strength and freedom when we lay down and expose our sins before God's awesome presence. Confession causes sin to lose its grip on us and its influence over our lives as it is revealed and acknowledged. True repentance does not blame circumstances or anybody else on but openly admits, "It was me and I am guilty." It is there when we honestly confess our sin that we give God space to begin the inner healing that we all so desperately need. My experience is that our confession can even heal what others have done to us. Honesty before God works wonders in our lives. There is an amazing freedom if we dare to confess before God our bitterness, our hatred, our envy and our greed that we may have felt towards others.

There is, however, another dimension of repentance in words that often terrifies us, and that is confessing our sins to other people. Within the Christian tradition, confession to a priest or a pastor is a well-used way of confessing sin. I have often seen in ministry time and in pastoral care the power of naming sin and the liberty and deliverance that that can bring. I have at times, quite literally seen burdens being lifted off someone and how the person stands up with a sense of being several kilos lighter. In the first church there was a place for the repentance in words by mouth. James writes that we should confess our sins to each other ( James 5:16), but I wonder how that confession really looked. What does a church look like where we really make time for confession? Confession before a priest in an anonymous confession booth only became part of the Catholic Church in the 13th century. In the first congregation, it was probably rather in communion with each other that this confession in words took place. The German priest and theologian Dietrich Bonhoeffer puts his finger on how important this confession is when he writes:

> "Sin demands to have a man by himself. It withdraws him from the community. The more isolated a person is, the more destructive will be the power of sin over him, and

the more deeply he becomes involved in it, the more disastrous is his isolation. Sin wants to remain unknown. It shuns the light. In the darkness of the unexpressed it poisons the whole being of a person." (Life Together and prayerbook of the Bible, Page 110)

We need to regularly bring our sin out into the light and walk honestly and humbly without becoming defensive. Sometimes pride or fearing what others think of us can stop us from the way of honesty. We like to keep up the facade where we think that our sin is our own business and that it doesn't affect others, but sin places itself between me and God. Dietrich Bonhoeffer, like so many others, have the experience that verbal confession is needed for sin to lose its final power over us. However, I am not a big proponent of public confession of private sins, but to confide in a Christian sister or brother is an important part of our repentance and a crucial part of our walk with Jesus.

We need to be sensitive and attentive when we speak with God, asking Him for wisdom and courage to know when it's time to seek help. That help can come through a Christian friend, a prayer group, a leader, or a pastor as we confess the sin that resides within us. We are called to support one another in following Jesus in every aspect of life, and for that, we need honest and sincere relationships. We need friends with whom we can be open, even to the point of revealing the dark secrets we all carry inside. Repentance, expressed in words, can wonderfully open the way for God's light and purity to shine into, and through, our lives.

## Repentance that leads to action

The repentance that begins in thought and is expressed in words must then result in deeds. When we in our board of elders talked about the Christian life as a journey, my friend Lennart Axklo told of his experience in regard to repentance. When he, as a young man, was about to be ordained as an evangelist God caught his attention. God reminded him of an incident a few years earlier when he had been poaching crayfish together with some friends. Together they had illegally taken 16 crayfish from a farmer's water. The day before his ordainment God's light shone with full force on this event. Eventually Lennart climbed into his car and together with his fiancé Marianne they set off to find the farmer in order to make things right before God. He was tense and nervous when he knocked on the door to pay for the illegally caught crayfish, and when the door opened he was met by a farmer who was, to say the least, very surprised. Lennart introduced himself, told the farmer what he had done, paid for the crayfish and then left the farm relieved to have done the right thing before God and man. God had tapped his heart and shown him something that he wanted Lennart to put right. Lennart readily admitted that there were far greater sins in his past, but it was this single event that God's Spirit had pointed to. For Lennart, his theft of crayfish was something that he needed to actively repent of before he could move on. The next day, his heart was at peace, and he was ready to be sent out as a worker in the kingdom of God.

I know just how easy it is to ignore these small calls to repentance, but it is in precisely these small choices that sets the course for a life of repentance. If God would let us see all our sin at the same time we would probably perish, but he often leads us to repent one sin at a time. This is where daily fellowship with the Holy Spirit is of prime importance. He is an expert in changing us from the inside out, and we need to give Him time and space to do that, also in our lives.

When Paul wrote his last letter, probably of four, to the church in Corinth, he mentioned that he, in an earlier letter, had been hard on them. He had rebuked the church, which he first regretted, but when he saw that the admonition led first to sorrow, then to repentance and finally to action Paul was glad (2 Corinthians 7:8-10). The result in Corinth was that they worked with longing and zeal for change so that they now acted differently (2 Corinthians 7:11).

As the founder of the Salvation Army, William Booth, aged 15, sat and listened as Isaac Marsden preached, he was suddenly struck by guilt for have stolen a silver pen from a schoolmate. This inner conviction did not let go and eventually William sought out his former classmate and admitted that he had wrongly acquired the pen and now wanted to return it. This act of repentance was the beginning of a time in William Booth's life where God began to use him powerfully in service building His kingdom and through him God ultimately changed the world.

Being honest and truthful in small details is an important part of repentance, and it is through repentance that our faith and trust in the Lord deepens and grows. By doing the right thing in smaller things our minds start that a journey of metamorphosis so that our very thoughts start being renewed. Repentance becomes a new way of life where we are transformed so that we start to bear the fruit of that repentance (Luke 3:8). John the

Baptist wanted to see this fruit in all those he baptized. When someone asked what this fruit was, John answered

> "Anyone who has two shirts should share with the one who has none, and anyone who has food should do the same. Then he told tax collectors not to collect any more than you are required to. To the soldiers he told them not to take advantage of their position to extort money and not to accuse people falsely." (Luke 3:7–14).

The fruit of repentance are the things that we do as a result of our thoughts being renewed and a result of the law of God being written on our hearts by the Holy Spirit. This will, in time, step by step, lead us to see the world and ourselves through God's eyes.

When the not-so-tall tax collector Zacchaeus was visited by Jesus at his home, he admitted that he had taken too much money from people. He did not say, "From now on I will act differently." Zacchaeus repented and decided, in that very moment, to repay fourfold all those from whom he had wrongfully taken money, and also to give half of his wealth to the poor. He realized that true repentance must result in action. Jesus' reaction to his repentance is quite remarkable, as He said: "Today salvation has come to this house" (Luke 19:1–10).

When we learn to do what we know is right, it helps us to follow Christ and to stay firmly on God's path. By being faithful in the little things, we deepen our relationship with God. Our repentance in practical works opens the way for us to live closer to God, which enables God to transform our lives. If we previously fiddled the numbers when submitting our tax returns, we may now find ourselves careful with the truth. If we used to lie we may find this become increasingly difficult. If we used to say nothing when a supermarket cashier forgot to scan an item so that we ended up paying less than we ought, we may now happily go back to pay the full amount in order to do what is right.

A consequence of knowing God is that we want to have the fruit of repentance in our lives. With Gods help we now strive for honesty, truth and generosity even if it costs us money, time, pride or convenience. It is in all the small, simple actions in everyday life that our faith becomes real. It is in the minor things that we get to see major stuff. It is not possible to go back in time and put every wrong right, but when God reminds us of a particular sin or wrong attitude, we better do our best to listen and obey. We do not do what is right in order so that God will love us, but because he already loves us (Romans 5:8). Sometimes disobedience can put God's work on hold in our lives, but God is patient and good and waits as He wants the fruit of repentance to be seen in us. Sometimes we must return a silver pen that we stole or go back to the store to pay for an item that we hadn't paid for. In doing so we can continue to walk on God's narrow road and not stop or get lost along the way. When we act on Gods word and let our repentance be expressed in deeds, sin starts to lose its power over us. In that way God gets an ever-greater space to work in our lives in his own way. And isn't that what we, deep down inside of us, really long for?

## The weight of sin

While I was growing up, in Ebenezer-Filadelfia church in Linköping, I would occasionally hear talk of something called the weight of sin. At the time I didn't know what the weight of sin was, but I associated it with crying and tears. When I have come across this same expression later in life and I have come to connect it more to a state where I understand more deeply that my sin has hurt God. Therefore, I grieve over the sin in my own life. Sorrow over sin in this way is nothing new. We can see such a pattern throughout the Bible. In Psalm 51, King David expresses this weight of sin when he write "my sin is always before me" (Psalms 51:3).

Later the prophet Isaiah saw the Lord sitting on His throne and bowed down in the presence of the living God. He wrote "Woe to me", I cried, "I am ruined! For I am a man of unclean lips, and I live among a people of unclean lips, and my eyes have seen the King, the Lord Almighty." (Isaiah 6:5).

Personally, I have rarely experienced that kind of overwhelming sense of guilt that some can testify to. It's not that I don't see my own sin, but that I prefer to see myself as forgiven rather than a sinner. As a Christian, God has made me righteous, purified me and adopted me as His child, which of course must awaken in me a gratitude and a jubilant and sincere joy. At the same time, it disturbs me that I am far too indifferent to the sin that exists in my own life. If I am honest, I most likely see my own sin as more of a human weakness, than as a rebellion against God. Maybe that's why I have had some difficulties with Psalm 51. In that song, David humbles himself, let's go of all his excuses, confesses his sin and repents. My problem with this psalm has not been David's confession but rather how he expresses himself later on. But to understand the context we first need to know something of the backstory. It was written by King David after he had committed adultery with Bathsheba, having previously had her husband, Uriah, killed. Nathan the prophet then goes to David, knocks on his door and points out in no uncertain terms exactly how the king of Israel has sinned. What always had felt a little strange to me is how David chooses to express himself to God in prayer after this. He says, "Against you, you only, have I sinned and done what is evil in your sight?" (Psalm 51:4).

In my opinion it was against Bathsheba that David sinned, and also against Uriah. Perhaps we can argue that he has sinned against his people and abused the trust they had put in him. But here David clearly states that it is "only" against God that he has sinned? How so? From Gods point of view, sin is first and foremost something that we do against our God, our creator. Of course, our sin can hurt, and harm other people and we must never think that we can ignore seeking forgiveness and reconciliation with the people that we have hurt. However, there is something here that needs to be awakened, a sorrow for what sin does to our relationship with God and a regret for how much hurt our sin causes God. "Godly sorrow that brings repentance" is what we need (2 Corinthians 7:10), and to live life even closer to our beloved Jesus. The author of Hebrews encourages us to do just that when he or she writes: "let us strip off every weight that slows us down, especially the sin that so easily trips us up" (Hebrews 12:1, NLT)

Over the years I have wrestled with the theology of repentance and have finally ended up at the same place that King David did.

If God exists, and if we are created through him and for him, it is first and foremost God to whom we are responsible. We need to realize that when we use our minds, mouths or hands to think, say or do something other than that which God has created us to do, we miss God's goal for our lives and that hurts God and it is this, in essence, that the Bible calls sin.

The prodigal son expressed this kind of repentance when he said: "I have sinned against heaven and against you" (Luke 15:21). It is when this heavenly dimension enters our lives that we can find our way back home. The gospel is the good news that the bad news no longer applies to us, that we no longer need to walk astray. God gives us new birth, "if anyone is in Christ, the new creation has come: the old has gone, the new is here!" (2 Corinthians 5:17). Therefore, we can confidently agree with John who says that "now we are children of God" (1 John 3:2).

New thoughts of repentance, like so much else in the Christian faith, are twofold; they involve both God and us. We start thinking in new ways as God renews our minds. What is important to God starts to become what is important to us. For this reason, it is crucial that we do our part and allow our minds to be renewed, by allowing God to speak to us through His word. At the same time, we believe in a living and active God who can and wants to transform and renew our thoughts so that we can understand more and more what His perfect will is (Romans 12:2). Repentance is not something that we will ever stop doing this side of eternity, instead daily repentance is an ongoing work as we more and more start to think God's thoughts. This is the door to a natural, supernatural life in God's presence, where God is glorified as repentance leads to thoughts, which leads to words which leads to actions.

# Chapter 6

## A FAITHFUL FAITH

"Without faith it is impossible to please God."
Hebrews 11:6

The next step on the path to salvation is faith. You are probably wondering why faith isn't the first step on the path and why it doesn't come before repentance. After all, "without faith it is impossible to please God" (Hebrews 11:6). That is true, if by faith we only mean believing in the existence of God. "Because anyone who comes to him must believe that he exists and that he rewards those who earnestly seek him" (Hebrews 11:6). But biblical faith is so much more than the simple belief that there is a God. Both the Old and New Testaments describe faith more as trust and a confidence in that God is who he says he is. Such faith requires that we first have a personal relationship with Him and to have that, we first need to have repented. As we are going to see in this chapter faith is more like faithfulness or to trust. To be more clear about what biblical faith is, we could say that faith has four sides, just like a box, where each side is equally important for our faith to be strong, grounded, sustainable and lifegiving.

## A faith rooted in history

The first side of the box is *the historical faith*, and by that I mean that it is possible to believe in a real, tangible God who has stepped into our world and has become part of our history. We can, with logical reasoning, argue for the existence of God and for belief in that He is the ultimate reason for everything. Thit is to believe that there is a God. Historical faith also means that we believe that God is who the Bible says he is. That he created the earth, that he led the people of Israel out of Egypt and most importantly, that Jesus has lived, died and risen from the dead. We can learn more and more about our history, through ancient findings and archaeological excavations and the Bible is constantly being strengthened in its historical reliability. The historical evidence supporting the Bible has never been stronger than it is today. Probably the most debated, and at the same time the most researched, event in all of ancient history are the events surrounding Jesus' death, burial, and resurrection. No other parts of the Bible have been more scrutinized than these, save for the story of creation. Many who have tried to disprove Jesus' death and resurrection have themselves become Christian when they realized that the evidence for the resurrection rest squarely on reliable historical facts. Lord Darling, who was formerly Attorney General of England, said:

> "There is so much and convincing evidence both of fact and circumstance, that no serious jury in the world could pass any other verdict than that the story of the resurrection is true." (Nicky Gumble, *Questions of Life*).

Jesus' death, burial and resurrection are historical facts that can be studied and researched. When faith becomes historical, it is no longer based on feelings, because historical faith is not based on experiences but rather on the historical facts and historical proof. Historical faith is therefore both stable and durable. When we find ourselves in periods of doubt and trials, we need historical faith as our foundation and anchor. We meet this kind of argument in the letters of the New Testament when, for example, Paul writes in his letter to the church in Corinth that they can actually ask any of the five hundred brothers who saw the resurrected Jesus at the same time, and that most of these eyewitnesses are still alive (1 Corinthians 15:6). Personally speaking, I see myself as a rational and logical thinker, and so apologetics and historical reliability have always been extremely important to my faith. Finding out the veracity of the biblical events has helped me to have greater faith in the Bible as a whole. For me, the arguments for God as Creator have also strengthened and deepened my faith. On top of that, philosophical and logical reasoning, as well as geological proofs, have led me to an even stronger faith in Gods existence. But to be a Christian is not merely to believe in God's existence. We must realize that our faith in God cannot be built solely on historical evidence; it must complete the longest half-meter journey in the universe - from the brain to the heart. This leads us to the second side of the Christian faith.

## A faith that is personal

To say that our faith needs to be *personal* means that we have come to realize that God not only loves the whole world, but that He also loves each one of us individually. We are invited into a personal relationship with God himself. He loves us even though we were lost in sin (Romans 5:8) and He wants to get to know us. In a personal faith like this, we move from simply believing in God's existence to having a personal relationship with Him. It is this personal trust and total surrender that Jesus repeatedly talked about when he called us to get to know God as our Father and to trust in Him with everything. Close, personal faith like this reaches its climax when, like Jesus, we can pray: "Not my will, but yours be done" (Luke 22:42). Like all relationships, a personal faith like this requires us to be actively speaking with God and to include Him as we go about our lives. Ultimately, personal faith is being able to say "I know that God exists, I spoke to him earlier today!"

The path to a personal faith can look different from person to person. When Paul and Silas came to Philippi, they met three people who each had a personal faith, even though their path to faith looked different. In the Acts 16, we find the story of Lydia, a business-woman with her own enterprise. Then there's a slave girl who was possessed by an evil spirit, and finally a jailer. These three people probably became the foundation of the first church in Philippi. Lydia, a merchant of purple cloth, was one of the women that Paul had spoken to down by the river. Paul and Silas looked for a place of prayer but instead they found an opportunity to share the gospel. Lydia is described as godly and was in all probability Jewish. She had a faith and a knowledge of the one true God, and in conversation with Paul she became convinced of the truth of his words. Lydia and her whole household were then baptized in the name of Jesus Christ. She met the Lord through knowledge and conversation and God opened her heart so that she accepted Him as Lord (Acts 16:14).

The slave girl, on the other hand, got to meet God through divine intervention. In the name of Jesus, Paul freed her from a spirit by which she predicted the future. There was no discussion, but sometimes God just steps right into our lives, as He did with Paul on the Damascus Road. When Paul, in the name of Jesus, commanded the demon to leave the girl, she was instantly delivered. The girl's owners became very angry as they realized that they could no longer make money through her ability. Lastly, there is the jailer who was tasked with guarding Paul and Silas while they were in prison. The jailer came to a personal faith when he encountered God's love through Paul and Silas. After a violent earthquake caused the prison doors to fling wide open, the jailer tried to take his own life as he thought that the prisoners had escaped. But Paul called out, "Do not harm yourself! We are all here (Acts 16:18b). The jailer may have been present a few hours earlier when Paul and Silas were whipped, but in Paul he saw God's love who didn't want to see the jailer hurt himself. After Paul shared with him the good news about Jesus he and his whole household were baptized. When Paul later writes a letter to Lydia, the jailer and perhaps also the slave girl, he begins his letter with the words "To all God's holy people in Christ Jesus at Philippi" (Philippians 1:1). God invites all of us to come to know Him as Lord, personally. Personal faith is not so much about believing in some doctrine or holding a certain theological position as the truth. In personal faith we get to spend time with God daily. With that said, theology and doctrine are still important; it is through the Bible that we understand who God is. It is through His word that He reveals himself to us, and most clearly in and through the incarnation of Jesus. In Psalm 73, we have the most fantastic expression of personal faith through the words of the psalmist Asaph: "Whom have I in heaven but you? And earth has nothing I desire besides you." (Psalms 73:25). Faith never stops at only acknowledging God's existence; it must lead to a relationship with God as Lord, Master, Father and Friend. In this psalm, Asaph expressed his personal faith in words, which brings us to the third side of faith.

DAY
18

## A faith expressed in words.

The third side of faith that I want to highlight is the *verbal faith*, meaning the faith that we express with our words. Paul does not hold back when he talks about the importance of expressing our faith verbally. He even says that the spoken faith is a central and important part of our walk with the Lord and that it even is a crucial part of our salvation. He writes "If you declare with your mouth, "Jesus is Lord," and believe in your heart that God raised him from the dead, you will be saved." (Romans 10:9). If faith has become personal then our hearts should overflow with words, speaking loudly about all that God has done for us. Many a time have I sat with young people who claimed to believe in God and that they tried to liv life according to Christian values. What hurts me the most is to see that even though they believe that Jesus is real, their faith still hasn't really taken root. In some cases, I have felt the need to explain top those I was counselling the importance of proclaiming before God, people and the spiritual realm who it is that they belong to and who they believe in. When we do that, our faith is strengthened and our relationship with God is deepened.

"If you declare with your mouth, "Jesus is Lord," and believe in your heart that God raised him from the dead, you will be saved. For it is with your heart that you believe and are justified, and it is with your mouth that you profess your faith and are saved." (Romans 10:9–10).

Our words matter and God responds to our confession of faith. It is this power of our words that Jesus' younger brother James talks about when he in his short letter, points to the importance of how we use our words. The tongue can affect our lives and our surroundings and that is why he argues that we must be careful with our words and use them wisely. Words can build up, create and give life, but they can also curse, tear down and set things ablaze ( James 3:1–12). Words are more than just sounds that emanate from our mouths. Salomon writers "The tongue had the power of life and death, and those who love it will eat its fruit." (Proverbs 18:21). What comes out of our mouths should be an expression of our faith but not many of us can say that that is how we are most of the time. I sometimes use the prayer that King David prayed when he desperately poured out his heart before the Lord saying, "Set a guard over my mouth, Lord; keep watch over the door of my lips" (Psalm 141:3). The words we speak have more power over our circumstances than we often think. Use your words wisely and use them to build up not only your own faith but also the faith that is present in others. Paul had this in mind when he wrote: "Do not let any unwholesome talk come out of your mouths, but only what is helpful for building others up according to their needs, that it may benefit those who listen" (Ephesians 4:29).

## A faith expressed through deeds

The fourth and final side of the Christian faith is evident by the deeds that we do. This kind of practical faith should make us act according to our beliefs. This is really self-evident. If we believe that God can forgive us, shouldn't that lead us to seek His forgiveness? If we are convinced that God can heal the sick, shouldn't that compel us to pray for those who are ill? If we believe that Jesus is the only way to God, shouldn't that clearly lead us to tell others about Him? And if we are confident that God knows everything, we need in terms of food, drink, and clothing, isn't it only natural for us to stop worrying about the things we so often chase after? Our faith in an almighty and loving God should lead us to seek His kingdom and His righteousness above all else, letting everything else become secondary (Matthew 6:25–33). This is where things get hard, where the rubber hits the road. If faith never leads to action, we need to ask ourselves "How much faith do I have and do I really believe all that I say that I believe in?" When James wrote his short but challenging letter, he declared that faith without works is dead. In fact, he went as far as to say that it is faith expressed in action that saves us ( James 2:14). It is only when we let our faith become visible in what we do that it becomes a living faith. If we believe from the bottom of our hearts that God is who He says He is, I am convinced that our lives would be completely different. Although Paul states that we are not saved by works (Ephesians 2:8–9), I am convinced that both Paul and James are in complete agreement: faith is not the result of works, but a real, living faith should always be accompanied by deeds.

Craig Groeschel, the pastor of Lifechurch in Oklahoma, has written a book with a rather contradictory title called *The Christian Atheist*. In this book he describes Christians who believes in God but lives as if He doesn't exist. If we are honest, then we all risk ending up there one way or another. It can be applied to our relationships, how we handle money, how we prioritize our time or our commitments. Faith must be visible through what we do so that we do not live as though God does not exist. James makes this clear when he says:

> "My brethren, what good is it if someone claims to have faith but does not have works? Can't faith save him? If a brother or sister is without clothes and lacks food for the day, what good is it if one of you says, "Go in peace, keep warm and eat your fill," but do not give them what the body needs? So it is with faith: in itself, without works, it is dead." ( James 2:14-17).

Navid arrived at Immanuel Church a couple of years ago and struggled with Malmö's housing situation. Unable to find accommodation, he moved to Gothenburg to stay with friends but wished to return to Malmö. He knew that it would take a miracle for him to get a place of his own without first having been waiting for months or years in a public queue for an apartment. One day Navid read from the Gospel of John, namely John 14, where Jesus said "My Father's house has many rooms" and "that I am going there to prepare a place for you" ( John 14:2). Navid immediately realized that if Jesus can prepare rooms in heaven, then he must also be able to prepare rooms on earth. Eagerly he began to pray every day that Jesus would give him a place to live in Malmö. He had faith in that God is able to do whatever we ask of Him. For Navid, it was a no-brainer that the God that he had come to know and love was both capable and willing to give him a home. After praying like this for 20 days, God suddenly opened a door for him to sign a first-hand rental contract on an apartment in Malmö. When Navid told us about this miracle, he concluded by emphasizing that his God has power, and that God is good. This certainty had taken root in him as he had spent time in prayer with the Lord and put his faith and trust in Him. This is the kind of plain and simple faith that God wants to see in our lives.

If we want to have a faith that deepens and matures, we need to have all four sides of faith in place. We cannot only base our faith on any one of these sides but we desperately needs all four of them. With that said, there can be seasons in life where the emphasis is more on one side than on the others. We need to take an honest look in the mirror and examine how much faith and trust we have in the God that we say that we believe in. Let us not be content with a faith that stops at merely believing in the existence of God. Wherever we are on our journey, God always wants to lead us to the place where we trust him more and more. God is real, and we can trust Him fully because He wants what's best for us. God's ultimate goal is not, and never has been, to have a world full of people who simply believe that He exists. If that was the case then He would probably have done a lot of things very differently. Instead, God's ultimate goal is a world full of people who know Him, loves Him and trust in Him.

## Living by faith

When Adam and Eve broke their relationship with God, it was not primarily the actual deed that they performed that was the main problem. The problem had arisen earlier when they no longer trusted God and that led them to an act of disobedience. The serpent's cunning campaign of persuasion was not primarily aimed at getting them to eat of the fruit, but rather to make them doubt God's goodness when he said, "Did God really say…?" (Genesis 3:1). The first humans did not trust that God wanted the best for them and when the serpent said that they would become like God if they only ate of the fruit, the matter was settled: "We do not trust God", and therefore they ate of the fruit. Their faith, or rather the lack thereof, led them into action. Thus the problem was not only disobedience, but also unbelief. They did not trust God and what he had said to them, they began to reason and conclude that they must take matters into their own hands for everything to be as they desired. Their unbelief and the belief that we need to go our own way has haunted humanity ever since. We have difficulty trusting God and putting our faith in Him. This is also why God's goal throughout history has been to regain the trust and confidence of His children. He wants us to place our trust in Him and what He says. When Abraham enters the story, he was a man who had failed in many areas, but God saw his faith and that he had complete trust in Him. We read that Abraham believed, that is he trusted, in God and was therefore counted as righteous (Genesis 15:6). It was not his belief in the existence of God, but rather his faith and confidence in God as an all-good God that God saw in Abraham.

God wants His children to trust Him because that was the point at which sin entered into the world. Perhaps that is why Jesus told us so many times not to worry. He wants to see a faith where we trust that God provides for and takes care of us, just as he takes care of the birds and the lilies of the field (Matthew 6:24–34). This is probably also why Jesus spoke so much about money, because he knows that it is one pivotal point on which our trust is put to the outmost test. As humans we first want to create our own financial security and then we leave our contribution to God and His church, if there is anything leftover. But, when we learn to give first to God, we show that we trust that God is faithful and able to provide for our needs. How we manage our money really reveals who or what we have ultimately placed our faith in.

When God looks at the world, it is not first and foremost blind obedience that he wants, but faith. He wants His children to throw themselves into their Father's arms shouting: "Catch me!" He loves it when we trust that "Dad knows best". He wants us to believe that He is in control and that He can be trusted, even though the world around us is in chaos. It is this kind of faith that God longs to see in our lives, a faith that prays "not my will, but yours be done" (Luke 22:42). When we have this kind of faith we obey God and submit to him because we know that our Heavenly Father is a good and loving God.

When I read the Bible, I sometimes stop and wonder if Jesus really meant what he said? Many things that Jesus said make me think, "Is that really true?". It seems that Jesus seriously expects his followers to believe that, with God, anything can happen. He said things like "if you have faith as small as a mustard seed, you can say to this mountain, 'Move from here to there' and it will move" (Matthew 17:20-21) and "whoever believes in me will do the works I have been doing, and they will do even greater things than these," if we only have faith ( John 14:12 – 14). These words of Jesus create in me a deep longing, which only increases when I hear about other people who actually live this kind of radical faith, that I had more of this simple trust in God's power. There is something so attractive about seeing ordinary, children of God live with a simple, childlike faith in Jesus. Can you imagine walking through life and seeing God work through you every day? That with each passing day we become more and more like Jesus so that our life can be a light that shines in the darkness for everyone to see (Matthew 5:14)? That through our lives we can do good deeds so that people will praise our Father in heaven (Matthew 5:16)? Could there be anything greater or more important than that? Our Heavenly Father wants us to trust Him and express our trust by saying as Jesus said "not my will, but yours be done" (Luke 22:42). This is the ultimate test of faith: we count on God to be with us even though we don't know where the road will lead us, to trust in God even though we know that the road will take us through suffering and difficulty. It is that kind of faith that I need more of, a faith that is a simple trust that God is who he says He is, and that He will keep all His promises, that He will go with me on all the paths of life if I walk with Him.

## A faith that keeps on believing

Hiking always requires a certain measure of endurance, and when the apostle John speaks about our faith journey, he emphasizes the same need for perseverance. John not only walked with Jesus for three years on earth, but he continued to walk with God into old age. When John wrote his Gospel, he is the one who spoke more about faith and belief than any of the other Gospel writers. He uses the word *faith* a total of 98 times. The Greek word for faith *pisteuō* is, like the Hebrew word *ĕmûnâh*, synonymous with faithfulness. John consistently chose to write about faith using a grammatical term that in English is best described in the continuous present tense, that is that it is describes something that is ongoing. To get to the full meaning of John's understanding of the word, it is best expressed as "believe and go on believing". John also uses this same tense with other words, but always with the same purpose: to encourage us to remain faithful in our walk.

When John tells us the reason why he wrote his gospel, we read that I was "so that you will believe *(and go on believing)* that Jesus is the Messiah, the Son of God, and that by *(going on)* believing you may have *(and go on having)* life in his name." ( Joh 20:31, italics mine) When we read the Bible through this lens, even well-known verses take on new light, for example: "For God so loved the world that he gave his one and only Son, that whoever believes *(and goes on believing)* in him, shall not perish but have *(and go on having)* eternal life" ( John 3:16, italics mine). We have eternal life, not in ourselves, but in Christ Jesus. Therefore, we must remain in Jesus in order to have His eternal life. "Whoever has the Son has life; whoever does not have the Son of God does not have life." (1 John 5:12).

My personal conviction is that faith finds its greatest expression in our prayers. This is where we see what our faith really looks like. If we don't pray, then our faith is probably superficial, fragile and reduced to an intellectual theory, but if prayer is something that we can't live without, faith is probably also more active in our lives. It is in our prayers that our motives are revealed. Is it me, my life and my desires that are at the center of my prayers, or is it God, His life and His desires that are at the center? As we walk the road of salvation, prayer keeps us on the right course and is also what makes our faith grow. As a disciple, it is natural to pray as we realize that the life that He gives us cannot be lived in our own strength. God invites us to walk in the good works, which God prepared in advance for us to do (Ephesians 2:10). As pilgrims, God constantly leads us to take steps of faith, and these steps are often a real challenge for us. When Noah began building the ark, it was a giant leap of faith where his reputation was ruined over the course of many decades (Genesis 6:9-22). Moses risked his life when he went to Pharaoh with the words: "Let my people go!" (Exodus 5:1). Peter risked getting wet and humiliated when he jumped over the side of the boat to walk on the water toward Jesus (Mark 6:45-51). The way of salvation is a way of faith where in fellowship with God we are constantly encouraged to believe that He can do things that for us are impossible. God does not look primarily at our skills or gifts, He looks at our hearts and our desires and it is in prayer that our true faith is revealed. It is in our prayers that we can see how great and good we believe God to be. Isn't it so that we often live with a picture of a small, limited God who sometimes surpasses himself. Instead we should live with a picture of a great God "who is able to do immeasurably more than all we ask or imagine" (Ephesians 3:20).

Faith keeps us steady on the path with Jesus. Faith is more than mere belief, it's a deep, unwavering trust in our Father's goodness. Since God wants to see this kind of faith in us, He has given us both His Spirit to help us and His Word, the Bible. The importance of God's Word to our faith cannot be overemphasized. Reading it for yourself, or reading it with others, truly helps to build up our faith. Another great help is to listen to teachings and sermons that faithfully proclaim the Word of God. But in our day and age, there are so many voices competing with the words God is speaking to us, that we often can't hear clearly what He is saying. I often find myself giving this piece of advice: subtract and remove some of the voices the world is preaching through. Maybe you need a time without social media or a period without Netflix in order to turn up the volume from the word of God. It is also when we read God's word that the living Word of God, Jesus, is reveled. Paul hit bullseye when he said, "faith comes from hearing the message, and the message is heard through the word about Christ" (Romans 10:17). God's word, when it is read under the guidance of the Holy Spirit is one of the best ways to boost our faith. This is exactly what God told Israel when he told them how to live a life of trust in their God.

> "These commandments that I give you today are to be on your hearts. Impress them on your children. Talk about them when you sit at home and when you walk along the road, when you lie down and when you get up. Tie them as symbols on your hands and bind them on your foreheads. Write them on the doorframes of your houses and on your gates" (Deuteronomy 6:6-9).

Reading, thinking and meditating on the word of God are crucial for our faith and for our walk with Jesus Christ. And it is in God's word we most clearly see Jesus the perfect Word of God.

86

# Chapter 7

## BAPTISM IN WATER

"Repent and be baptized, every one of you, in the name of
Jesus Christ for the forgiveness of your sins."
Acts 2:38

The next crucial step on our walk with Jesus is baptism in water.
I honestly don't remember very much of my own baptism. I
know that I was nine years old and that it was my father who
baptized me and my brother Patric in Filadelfia church in
Linköping. When it was my turn, I stepped down into the water
and my dad lowered me completely under the surface. As far as
I can remember, nothing revolutionary happened at that
moment. I had no visions nor any revelations, but in actuality
everything was different. I had decided to follow Jesus and the
path that he had laid out for me. When we are submerged in the
water of baptism something greater happens than just that our
bodies getting wet.

Those of us who are members of churches that have their roots
in the revival of the 19th and 20th centuries often emphasize the
human side of water baptism. We sometimes say that in getting
baptized I am showing before God and people that I want to
follow Jesus and "never go back". But, as I read the Bible, I
realize with fascination that most of the verses that talk about
baptism don't mention at all, my choice or, what I want to say

with my baptism. Instead, God's Word emphasizes what He does when we get baptized in the name of the Father, the Son and the Holy Spirit. Just as in repentance and faith, baptism is something in which both God and man are active. Of course, baptism is also a confession and a clear, public statement of faith, but if it stops there then we are missing something important and decisive.

On the day of Pentecost, the people were so struck by Peter's message that they asked the disciples: "What shall we do?" Peter then replied with the words: "Repent and be baptized, every one of you, in the name of Jesus Christ for the forgiveness of your sins" (Acts 2:37-38). Baptism cleanses us from our sins. It can also be compared to the waters of the Red Sea that the people of Israel passed through when they fled from Egypt. The water separated the Israelites new, free life from their life of slavery in Egypt. On the other side of the sea something new was waiting, but soon they would discover that it was easier for God to get the people of Israel out of Egypt than to get Egypt out of the people of Israel. In the same way, we are set free from the slavery of sin through baptism, but as we also know, it is easier to get us out of sin than it is to get sin out of us. In his first letter, Peter uses the image of Noah's flood to explain that baptism saves us in the same way that the ark saved Noah and his family (1 Peter 3:20–21). In light of what we read in the Bible, baptism is much more than a confession, it is something far greater than mere symbolism. The water opens up an entirely new dimension, because in baptism we are united with Jesus Christ, and through the water, we can leave the slavery of sin behind us. The New Testament emphasizes baptism as a physical act with far-reaching spiritual consequences, one that leads us into a completely new life. Therefore, the Word of God repeatedly highlights the cleansing power of baptism, but even more so, it emphasizes baptism as a burial and a place where a resurrection takes place.

During my first seven years at Immanuel Church in Malmö, we baptized over 150 people in the name of Jesus Christ. The majority were from Iran and Afghanistan, and after completing an Alpha course, they were baptized to be united with Jesus. Whenever someone is baptized in our church we ask them to write down a few lines about the path that led them to Christ. This text is then read aloud as they step into the water. I'm just saying "WOW!" Seeing lives being transformed by Jesus is something one never gets tired of. It feels almost unreal to witness this miracle again and again and almost every time I find myself moved to tears.

## Baptism cleanses us

> "Get up, be baptized and wash your sins away, calling on his name." (Acts 22:16).

Normally, we step into the shower or sink down into the bathtub to wash away dirt or an unpleasant smell. It's somewhat strange how the dirt on the outside of our bodies tends to creep under the skin and affect our whole being, even our mood. When our body becomes clean, something happens to all of us. Many can testify that a shocking experience or traumatic event can drive a person to stand in the shower for hours, trying to wash away the trauma. It's as if we want to feel the outer cleanliness seep into us and make us clean on the inside as well. We are constantly reminded that we are created with a body, soul, and spirit, and that God desires to do His work in all of who we are. (1 Thessalonike 5:23). Baptism is, in a way, a cleansing bath which has consequences for the whole of life. We are washed clean from the sin that has soiled our lives and what a privilege it is to be able to wash away everything old, so that after being cleansed we can take our first steps on our lifelong walk with Jesus.

But what is the significance of baptism? Do you have to be baptized to go to heaven? Is baptism really that important? After all, the thief on the cross came to paradise without being baptized (Luke 2:39-43). Of course, baptism is not a magical act that saves in and of itself. But when we have repented and begun to walk in faith with God, baptism becomes the natural next step on our new path. Who does not want to be cleansed of sin and to have a clear conscience? God wants to give us the opportunity to start our walk with Him freshly washed and clean and with an assurance that the old is gone and that the new has come. (2 Corinthians 5:17)

## Baptism as a funeral

"Don't you know that all of us who were baptized into Christ Jesus were baptized into his death. We were therefore buried with him through baptism into death in order that, just as Christ was raised from the dead through the glory of the Father, we too may live a new life." (Romans 6:3-4)

Paul speaks of the fact that we, in baptism, have buried our old self and then risen together with Jesus. In other words, the baptismal water is doing more than just cleaning you, it is also your grave where your old sinful life has been buried. At the same time, it is your birthplace where you are born again into God's family.

When John the Baptist baptized people in the Jordan River, it was more than a ritual. It was considered a baptism of repentance, a clear sign that they had actively chosen to follow a new path in life. John's baptism was a baptism of repentance that would lead to new thoughts and a new way of looking at life. Occasionally we forget that Christian baptism is not the same as the baptism as John practices. Instead, Jesus introduced a new kind of baptism where we are actually baptized into his death. In baptism, we rise to new life together with Christ and it is God who plays the most active part in our baptism. For the Jews, both John's baptism and Christian baptism were awful stumbling blocks. Ancient Jewish writings show how a gentile convert could become a part of the Jewish people. One of the things that a new convert had to do was to shave their heads and then allow themselves to be washed completely clean in water. If a convert was a man, then he would also be circumcised. After this they were considered as natural-born Jews and from that day on they also celebrated a new birthday. When John and later Jesus' disciples began to baptize Jews, they signaled that God was about to call out a people fit for His new kingdom. This is why the authors of the Bible also emphasize how baptism gives us a new identity where we, through Jesus' death and resurrection, can become part of God's family, His people.

Thinking of baptism as a funeral is central to understand what it means to be baptized into the death of Jesus. In his letter to the Colossians, Paul writes that we were "buried with him in baptism" and that through baptism we have left our old lives behind (Colossians 2:12). Something definitive happens in this burial. The old man or woman, burdened with the weight of sin, is no longer there. Paul argues that this is how we should think of ourselves, in Christ we are "dead to sin but alive to God" (Romans 6:11). In Swedish the idea of baptism as a funeral is reinforced as we call the place of baptism, appropriately, dopgrav, *dop* meaning baptism and *grav* meaning grave. As we are burying our old selves something big and amazing is happening. We are also raised to a new life, a life in which we leave behind the kingdom of darkness and enters into the kingdom of God's beloved Son (Colossians 1:13). We are united in baptism with Jesus' death and resurrection where "the old has gone and the new is here" (2 Corinthians 5:17).

A person who has been baptized in faith can look back and boldly state "Satan, sin and death, you no longer have any power over me. "I am dead to sin but alive to God" (Romans 6:11). The devil, who is the ruler of this world, has lost his power over my life. To him, I am lost, but to God, I am found. Through baptism, I become a citizen of God's kingdom and a part of His new people, which is the church of the living God (1 Timothy 3:15). A people who are called "to go and make disciples of all nations, baptizing them in the name of the Father and of the Son and of the Holy Spirit" (Matthew 28:19).

## To walk in your baptism

"Repent and be baptized, every one of you, in the name of Jesus Christ for the forgiveness of your sins. And you will receive the gift of the Holy Spirit." (Acts 2:38).

Baptism is, like faith, a gift. As I said before, the majority of Bible verses to do with baptism are connected to the part that God plays in baptism. God takes this physical act and through it He works with His own tremendous strength and power. In the same way that eating the fruit of the Tree of the Knowledge of Good and Evil had disastrous consequences on our relationship with God, and in the same way that eating the Lord's Supper brings us into communion with Jesus Christ, baptism is a physical act in which God is active and has chosen to manifest Himself.

I was only 9 years old, as I previously wrote, when I was baptized on New Year's Eve, 1981. Sometimes I wish I had waited until I could better understand what I was doing, but I don't regret it. In some cases, years can pass by, between repentance and baptism, which raises many questions as we read the Bible. In the early church, repentance, faith and baptism belonged closely together at the start of a person's walk with our Lord. If we have been raised in the Christian faith, there is a great risk that we come to a faith in God without having truly repented. We might believe in Jesus, but he is not really our Lord and Master. But, without repentance, without turning away from sin, without making Jesus Lord and Savior, baptism becomes incomprehensible. In baptism, we have been set "free from the law of sin and death" (Romans 8:2) and our "life is now hidden with Christ in God" (Colossians 3:3).

Why then you might ask, was Jesus baptized? After all, he had no need to be forgiven of his sin. We must remember the baptism with which Jesus was baptized. John performed a baptism of repentance and Jesus, a citizen of Israel, identified himself with a people who needed to repent of sin. He then showed that he was a part of the new people of God that was about to take shape. John prepared the way and made people ready to enter into the kingdom of God which was drawing near. When John baptized Jesus, it heralded the start of Jesus' public ministry, to lead God's new people into his kingdom, a kingdom that is not of this world. When Jesus after his baptism broke the surface of the Jordan river, the Father confirmed that "This is my son, Whom I love; with him I am well pleased" (Matthew 3:17). At that moment the Holy Spirit descended upon Jesus and filled him with power. It was in the power of the Holy Spirit that Jesus lived the life that his Father had sent him to live and enabled him to do His will. Fully human, Jesus was completely depended on the guidance of the Holy Spirit and on his strength, power and gifts. Fully God, He was stripped of His divine privileges and "did not consider equality with God something to be used to His own advantage" (Philippians 2:6). Everything Christ did as a human being was done in complete dependence on the power and guidance of the Holy Spirit.

For us, things are different. We do not practice John's baptism of repentance but instead we are baptized into Jesus' death and resurrection. Through baptism we are born into God's kingdom. And when we, through the waters of baptism, are united with Jesus we become a part of God's people, and we are born again by His Holy Spirit who cries out from within us, that we also are God's beloved children (Romans 8:16). In baptism, we become part of God's church, his people, which is His own family. We must no longer see ourselves as individuals, as we are now a part of God's household (1 Timothy 3:15), and Jesus is our brother (Romans 8:29). The Spirit is God's precious gift to us, he is a sign or seal that declares that we are a part of God's new creation (2 Corinthians 1:22). The God who previously only filled the Holy of Holies in the temple, now has a new temple to live in, and that is us (1 Corinthians 3:16, 1 Corinthians 6:19). I don't think that we can ever really understand how great and awesome this is, that God not only is with us, but that he also is within us ( John 14:17). In other words, you will never, ever be alone.

# Chapter 8

## RECEIVE THE HOLY SPIRIT

"Repent and be baptized, every one of you, in the name of
Jesus Christ for the forgiveness of your sins.
And you will receive the gift of the Holy Spirit."
Acts 2:38

The Holy Spirit is truly a precious gift. The God who created the universe does not want to be a God from a distance, but a God who comes close to us. When the first Pentecost occurred 10 days after Jesus returned to the Father, this became the new reality. God was no longer separated from us but chose to take up his dwelling in us who believe. Thanks to the cross, we can receive forgiveness for our sins and become clean and purified. Through Jesus we are cleansed and that purification is what is necessary for God to be able to live in us with his own presence. Just as Jesus was filled with Holy Spirit, we his disciples are now God's new dwelling place here on earth. We are equipped by the very same power and love that also filled Jesus. Not only that, but there is also a bond between disciples that unites us and makes us part of God's great family. When Peter spent time with John, it was not just John that Peter met with, but also with God who lived in John. God is now present among his people by his Spirit. When we repent, believe in Jesus and are baptized, we can receive God's Holy Spirit as a gift, as a deposit guaranteeing that we one day will share in the eternal hope that lies ahead of us (Ephesians 1:13 –14). For the first followers of Christ, life in the Spirit naturally follow on from being baptized in water. For Peter, Gods presence in him through the Holy Spirit was the highlight and that made him say: "Repent and be baptized, every one of you, in the name of Jesus Christ for the forgiveness of your sins. And you will receive the gift of the Holy Spirit." (Acts 2:38). God wants to give every newborn believer the best gift in the world, his own presence. We do not receive the Spirit as a reward for long and faithful service. John, who baptized with water, said of Jesus that "he will baptize you with the Holy Spirit and fire" (Luke 3:16). Jesus himself said that the Spirit will be like a spring of water that never dries up ( John 7:37-38).

For a long time I have wondered at what point on our journey do we receive the Spirit as a gift and if that is different to being baptized in the Spirit. What happens when we repent and what happens when we are filled with the Spirit? The more I think and read about it, I realize that these are not simple questions. During my preparation for this book, I was talking to several of my friends and fellow pastors. One evening I got a notification that I had received a text message. It was from my friend Johan, who wrote a short and concise answer to my question. This is what he wrote: "Jesus was conceived by the Holy Spirit yet the Spirit still needed to fill Jesus before he could begin his public ministry." Of course, there is always a risk in finding a simple explanation to describe something comp-licated. But images can still help us to put words to our faith. In a way, we can say that when we repent, believe and get baptized, we are conceived and born of the Spirit, we are made righteous and now belong to God. At the same time, the Spirit needs to fill us even more so that we are empowered to live the new life that he wants us to live. To walk as a Christian without being constantly filled by the Spirit is like being a car without gas or like a vacuum cleaner without electricity. Hopefully you've never tried vacuuming an entire house without plugging the power cord into the wall. In that case, you would be working hard without having succeeded in anything other than pushing the dirt and dust around in front of you. The Spirit is what makes all the difference. Of course, we are born again by the Spirit when we repent, believe in Jesus as Lord and get baptized. But we need to be baptized and filled with the Spirit to be able to live the life God has intended us to live.

Even though I was born of the Spirit and am a child of God, there is a dimension of the Holy Spirit that I long to have more and more of. When we read about the Holy Spirit in the New Testament, we cannot get any other understanding than that all those who received the Spirit knew that they had experienced something out of the ordinary. Therefore, when Paul came to Ephesus, his first question was: "Did you receive the Holy Spirit when you believed?" (Acts 19:2). They didn't know what he meant, so he asked them: "Than what baptism did you receive? "John's baptism," they replied" Then everything became clear to Paul and he said:

> "John's baptism was a baptism of repentance. He told the people to believe in the one coming after him, that is, in Jesus. On hearing this, they were baptized in the name of the Lord Jesus. When Paul placed his hands on them, the Holy Spirit came on them, and they spoke in tongues and prophesied." (Acts 19:1-6).

For me personally, there has been a definite danger that I have so strongly emphasized the work of the Holy Spirit in regeneration that I have neglected to speak of the possibility of being filled with more of the life and power of the Holy Spirit. Being baptized in water is an event that we can be sure, beyond a shadow of a doubt, that we have gone through. In the same way, it seems that in the book of Acts the same was true of the baptism of the Holy Spirit. The Spirit is so much more than a silent, passive, divine presence in our lives. The Spirit wants to speak to us, lead us, work in us and redeem his gifts in us so that He, the Spirit, manifests in us for the common good (1 Corinthians 12:7). The Bible is crystal clear on this point, that there is always more of God's Spirit that we can experience. God is calling us to allow ourselves to be continually filled by the Holy Spirit. As we live life in the Spirit, God gives us an inner conviction of who we are. "The Spirit himself testifies with our spirit that we are God's children" (Romans 8:16).

## Limping through life

Sadly, there are many Christians who are limping through life without having received power from on high. Many are also tired and sweaty from having vacuumed their whole house without the power cord plugged in. Often, I have heard how Christians think it is heavy and difficult to serve God, how they toil away without results. I have often thought about how often we vacuum without having plugged the vacuum in. The Holy Spirit gives us power and strength, he helps and comforts us, he wants to guide and help us pray. It is this wonderful gift of God that makes all the difference. The Swedish denomination

*Evangelical Free Church*, of which I am a part, states in its statement of faith and beliefs:

> "Without the Holy Spirit, God is distant, Christ remains in the past, the Gospel becomes empty words, the Church is merely an organization, mission turns into propaganda, worship becomes group therapy, and the Christian life is reduced to slave morality."

Sadly, there are some of us that nod in recognition, as we have all, at some point, experienced that sense of "withoutness." But with the Holy Spirit, God is near, Christ is alive and present, the Gospel is powerful and transformative, the Church is a living community, mission is an authentic witness to a world that is lost and broken, worship is a true encounter with God, and the Christian life is one of freedom and grace.

If we fail in helping each other to live our lives with God's Holy Spirit, we leave each other forgiven and clean for sure, but still empty. We need to guide new disciples to be filled with God's power from on high so that we do not deprive them of the Helper that God wants to give them. It is therefore encouraging to read about the lives of the first disciples. They had repented, they believed in Jesus, were baptized in water and they were then filled with the Holy Spirit. But although they had received the Spirit we can read that "the disciples were filled with joy and with the Holy Spirit." (Acts 13:52). As pilgrims on the way of salvation, we are conceived and born by the Spirit and "since we live by the Spirit, let us keep in step with the Spirit." (Galatians 5:25). We need the Spirit to be able to live our lives according to God's good will. On top of that, there is a strong emphasis in both Jesus' teaching and the teaching of the first church that

God's Spirit does not only want to do a work *in* us but also *through* us. Jesus said "you will receive power when the Holy Spirit comes on you; and you will be my witnesses in Jerusalem, and in all Judea and Samaria, and to the ends of the earth." (Acts 1:8). The Spirit was not given to the church so that we can soak in God's presence and keep him to ourselves, but as a power from on high to equip us to go out into the whole world and make disciples of all nations (Acts 1:8).

The Spirit is a gift that we need to ask for and actively choose to seek and receive. After all, we are commanded to "be filled with the Spirit" (Ephesians 5:18). But the Spirit does not force himself on anyone, he waits for us to allow him to fill us. His presence is the power that we need on the journey that we have in front of us. In one of Jesus sermons he said:

> "So I say to you: Ask (*and keep on asking*) and it will be given to you; seek (*and keep on seeking*) and you will find; knock (*and keep on knocking*) and the door will be opened to you. For everyone who asks receives; the one who seeks finds; and to the one who knocks, the door will be opened. "Which of you fathers, if your son asks for a fish, will give him a snake instead? Or if he asks for an egg, will give him a scorpion? If you then, though you are evil, know how to give good gifts to your children, how much more will your Father in heaven give the Holy Spirit to those who ask him!"

> (Luke 11:9–13, my emphasis).

I long to see churches where we, together, pray, seek, and strive to live in God's holy presence, churches where we, as God's children, long to be filled more and more with the Holy Spirit, so that God becomes increasingly visible in us. It is good to remind ourselves that a large part of Jesus' life and ministry was to be active in the power and gifts of the Spirit. Through the power of the Spirits he performed healing, gave prophetic words and words of knowledge, which many times renewed the wonder and longing of the people who met Jesus. If we want to be disciples of Jesus, we need to walk together with God's presence through His Spirit and in the same power and supernatural life as Jesus did.

## The Spirit as our helper

DAY 23

"And I will ask the Father, and he will give you another advocate to help you and be with you forever the Spirit of truth. The world cannot accept him, because it neither sees him nor knows him. But you know him, for he lives with you and will be in you." ( John 14:16–17).

There are many names in the Bible to describe the Holy Spirit. One that Jesus himself uses several times is the word helper or comforter (*parakletos),* which means "one called to stand by our side" ( John 14:16, 14:26, 15:26 16:7). The word can also be translated advocate, such as a defense lawyer who represents a defendant in a court of law. Isn't it remarkable that when Jesus left his disciples, he arranged everything so that they would not have to be alone. The words *another helper* actually mean *a helper of the same kind.* In the same way that Jesus had been their helper, he now asks the Father to send another Helper just like him. Jesus actually goes as far as to say that the Holy Spirit will even be a better helper to them than he has been, because the Spirit will not only be with them but also in them ( John 14:17).

The first thing the Holy Spirit does is to help us in our relationship with the Father. Together with our spirit, he testifies that we are children of God (Romans 8:16). He also helps us to pray when we do not know what to pray for (Romans 8:26). It is the Holy Spirit who is God's active presence in our lives and when we spend time with God, it is through the Spirit that this fellowship take place. The Holy Spirit also helps us to remember what Jesus has said, and the Spirit will also remind us of the truth ( John 16:13) so that we can see more clearly who Jesus is and what God's will is.

The second thing that the Holy Spirit does is to let his thoughts change our worldview. He helps us to see ourselves and others through God's eyes. The Spirit is the one who transforms us from deep within and who renews us so that we understand how we can walk the life that God has created us to walk. Standing in front of the mirror and trying to see ourselves with God's eyes is often difficult. We are not one with our failures, our shortcomings or our sins. Nor are we what others say about us. Ultimately, it is what God says about us that really matters. When the Spirit descended on Jesus at His baptism, the Father spoke from heaven and said, "This is my Son, whom I love; with Him I am well pleased" (Matthew 3:17). As God's chosen and called, these words are true for us as well: we are God's beloved daughters, we are God's beloved sons, and *we are His handiwork, created in Christ Jesus to do good works, which God prepared in advance for us to do"* (Ephesians 2:10). My longing is that God would look at me and be well pleased. My prayer is that I will one day hear His words: *"Well done, good and faithful servant!"* (Matthew 25:23). Although we often fall back into seeing ourselves through human eyes, God's Spirit wants to be our helper, so that we may learn to see what our Heavenly Father sees in us. God's ultimate goal is that we would be *"conformed to the image of His Son, that He might be the firstborn among many brothers and sisters"* (Romans 8:29).

The third thing that Gods Holy Spirit helps us with, is to actively live out our faith so that others can see who lives in us. We are His masterpiece, created through Christ Jesus to do (to walk in) the good works to which God from the beginning ordained us (Ephesians 2:10). Living life, the way God wants us to live is impossible without the Holy Spirit, "for it is God who works in you to will and to act in order to fulfill his good purpose." (Philippians 2:13). In the same way that the Holy Spirit filled Jesus and was an active force in his life, the Holy Spirit wants to fill us and help us to live like Jesus. In Jesus' conversation with His disciples just before the cross, He emphasized the importance of receiving the Holy Spirit. It is in this same discourse that Jesus tells His followers, *"Whoever believes in me will do the works I have been doing, and they will do even greater things than these, because I am going to the Father."* ( John 14:12) And we know what happened—when Jesus returned to the Father, the Holy Spirit was poured out. *"Unless I go away,"* said Jesus, *"the Advocate will not come to you."* ( John 16:7). We are called, just like Jesus, to be filled with the Spirit and to do all that God has sent us to do.

## The Spirit who brings forth fruit

"But the fruit of the Spirit is love, joy, peace, forbearance, kindness, goodness, faithfulness, gentleness, and self-control." (Galatians 5:22-23a).

In the amazing letter that Paul sent to the church in Galatia he paints a picture of two kinds of life. One kind of life that is lived out of a broken and sinful nature (Galatians 5:19–21). This kind of life is one that we are all far too familiar with. We all struggle in one way or another with pride, greed, lust, impurity or anger. The amazing thing is that immediately after the description of life in the flesh, Paul describes another kind of life to show what life in the spirit can be like (Galatians 5:22-24). He speaks of the Spirit as someone who makes us bear fruit. In nature, fruit is the result of a bee, or other insect, moving pollen from one flower to another. When pollination takes place, the wonderful process of turning a flower into fruit begins. It is a wonderful picture that describes what the Spirit does when he comes from the Father into our lives and pollenates. Then the fruit can begin to grow in us. Fruit is not the result of striving or toiling, but the result of being pollinated by the Spirit of God. He wants to work within us. That is why time in the presence of God is of the highest importance.

An interesting detail that we can find in the letter to Galatians is that Paul uses the word fruit in its singular, not plural, form. It's not about nine different fruits, but rather one fruit with nine different flavors. I don't know about you, but I have often looked at Paul's list of the fruit and been quite pleased to be able to tick some of the flavors on my list. However, I have seen other flavors as a bigger challenge and it is easy to think that our spiritual health should not be measured based on which flavor we have the most of, but on which flavor we have the least of. If the fruit of the Spirit is a single fruit and not nine different ones, a lack of taste should make us desperately seek God so that we can see more of the Spirit's fruit in our lives. Paul flips this around and wants us to desire more of God's fullness and life. When the Spirit fills us, it should result in our shortcomings and weaknesses being transformed, making us look more and more like Jesus. If it is God's will and goal to conform us to the image of His Son, then we should hunger for and strive to put ourselves in a position where God, who is a good and loving God, can pollinate us through His Spirit. And He does so for a purpose: so that our lives may glorify Him as the fruit of the Spirit begins to grow in us. Sometimes, fruit can feel a little sour or hard, but over time it ripens and becomes increasingly sweet. It should be a lesson to all of us not to stress or lose patience. As our thoughts are being renewed, we can live in faith, that the fruit of the Spirit will start to make God visible in our lives. As we more and more allow ourselves to be filled by the Spirit, the fruit can grow and ripen until it finally tastes delicious with all of its nine different flavors.

It is likely that Paul based his entire idea of fruit on what Jesus taught His disciples shortly before He was crucified. In John's Gospel, Jesus says:

> "I am the vine; you are the branches, If you remain in Me and I in you, you will bear much fruit; apart from Me you cand do nothing. If you do not remain in Me, you are like a branch that is thrown away and withers; such branches are picked up, thrown into the fire and burned." (John 15:5-6)

Our part is to remain in Jesus by living close to him through the Spirit of God. The Spirit is our helper but also the one who brings us God's own presence and life. After speaking about the fruit of the Spirit Jesus pleads with us to receive the Spirit as our helper and after Paul talked about the fruit of the Spirit he pleads with us to *"keep in step with the Spirit"* (Galatians 5:25). The Spirit is the world's best travelling companion on the road to salvation, and it is an indescribable privilege to walk through life with him. By abiding in Jesus and walking in step with the Spirit, his fruit finds the best conditions in which to grow in order that we will be filled with more love, joy, peace, patience, kindness, goodness, faithfulness, humility and self-control.

## The Spirit as the giver of gifts

> "Now to each one the manifestation of the Spirit is given for the common good. To one there is given through the Spirit a message of wisdom, to another a message of knowledge by means of the same Spirit, to another faith by the same Spirit, to another gifts of healing by that one Spirit, to another miraculous powers, to another prophecy, to another distinguishing between spirits, to another speaking in different kinds of tongues, and to still another the interpretation of tongues. All these are the work of one and the same Spirit, and he distributes them to each one, just as he determines."

(1 Corinthians 12:7-11)

It's easy to think of Jesus when we read about the various gifts that the Spirit gives. We see how Jesus functioned in most of these gifts, just as he had all the nine different flavors of the fruit of the Spirit clearly visible in is life. But God doesn't only give us his Spirit to make us more like Jesus in terms of character. He also wants us to do the things that Jesus did. The gifts of the Spirit are the toolbox that we can use so that people can understand who God is and experience what He is like. For example, by functioning in the gift of healing it becomes clear that God is our physician. Through words of knowledge we understand that God not only knows us but knows everything about us. God's wisdom can be revealed as we function in the gift of imparting wisdom to others. But these gifts are not for a small exclusive band of faithful disciples. The key in the text above is the words "to each one". I really love that, it signals that in a certain context, God can use "each one" of us to function in the gifts that He gives us. The gifts belong to Him, and without His Spirit there are no gifts. When we have received the Holy Spirit, the potential exists in us all to function in any of these different gifts as he sees fit (1 Corinthians 12:7, 11). If healing, wisdom, or a prophetic word is needed, the Spirit can knock on the door of our hearts and say, "Today you need to be useful in My kingdom with My gifts." Through His fruit and His gifts, God conforms us so that we can be mediators of His character and His power, a power that can transform people's lives as they see Christ in us.

As always, when we read the Bible, we must understand each verse and chapter in its context. Chapters 12 and 14 of Paul's first letter to the church in Corinth, must be understood in this way. In chapter 12 Paul writes about the gifts of the Spirit, then he goes on to explain how the members of the church should think of themselves as part of a body, without rank or competition. He then talks about God's love in chapter 13 before returning in chapter 14 to the gifts and how they should be used when the members of the church meet together. I love how Paul, in between discussing the gifts of the Spirit in chapters 12 and 14, emphasizes radical, outgiving selfless love in chapter 13. We are to seek God's gifts, not so that we can make ourselves look good or to show how godly we are, but so that we put them to good use in His kingdom and demonstrate and express His love.

Let us never speak about the gifts without also speaking about love. Paul wrote,

> "If I speak in the tongues of men or of angels, but do not have love, I am only a resounding gong or a clanging cymbal. If I have the gift of prophecy and can fathom all mysteries and all knowledge, and if I have a faith that can move mountains, but do not have love, I am nothing. If I give all I possess to the poor and give over my body to hardship that I may boast, but do not have love, I gain nothing. Love is patient, love is kind. It does not envy, it does not boast, it is not proud. It does not dishonor others, it is not self-seeking, it is not easily angered, it keeps no record of wrongs. Love does not delight in evil but rejoices with the truth. It always protects, always trusts, always hopes, always perseveres." (1 Corinthians 13:1-7).

It is my firm belief that gifts without love at their core are unbiblical.

In his gospel the disciple John tells us why Jesus came to Earth. He wrote "For God so loved the world that he gave his one and only Son, that whoever believes in him shall not perish but have eternal life." ( John 3:16). We can also apply his word to the gifts of the Spirit. For God so loved the world that He gave prophecy, healing, miracles, faith, and knowledge to His body, so that the world would not perish but have eternal life as they come to know who Jesus is. As a congregation, we need to eagerly seek the gifts of the Spirit (1 Corinthians 14:1) so that we can better show the world who God really is. We must never forget that we are here on Earth with a calling and a mission, that the world might be saved through Jesus. We are equipped by the gifts of the Spirit but our character is changes by the fruit of the Spirit. Just think what an incredible grace this is, that despite our brokenness and weakness we can still be an instrument of God's love. In us lives the same Spirit that raised Christ Jesus from the grave (Romans 8:11).

I long for us to pray for the sick with ever greater boldness and for God's church to live in the jubilant and sincere joy that we only can find in Him. Sometimes I wonder if we really understand what a wonderful helper we have received when God gave us his Holy Spirit. We no longer have to walk in our own strength, and never again do we have to walk alone. God's Holy Spirit must be in us like rivers of living water that do not dry out ( John 7:38-39). So, let us eagerly seek to be bearers of God's fruit, and let us also eagerly seek the gifts He wants to give us. What gifts do you long to function in? Talk to God about them and pray persistently that He will give them to you and make them visible in your life. Perhaps you should seek out a person who already is functioning in the gifts that you long for and ask them to lay their hands upon you. As Jesus said, "Freely you have received; freely give" (Matthew 10:8). In 2011, I received such a gift when I was at a conference that was focused on healing. There was a lot of good teaching during those days and some other things that passed me by, but I longed to be used in the gift of healing. When I came home to Falun again, I realized that something had happened to me, I had brought something home with me that I didn't have before. It felt like I had been infected with the gift of healing and I saw how God had done something tangible and new in me. The following weekend I saw three concrete healings: a lump on the side of the ribs that disappeared, a knee that miraculously became well and a foot that suddenly stopped hurting.

I long for God's people to see more of His power. We need to boldly lay hands on those whom we baptize so that they will be filled with the Holy Spirit. We need to pray that they will come to know God personally and be equipped for service in His kingdom. People's eternity is at stake, and it is when we are filled with the life of the Spirit it is then that His love will be seen in us.

## Be filled with the Spirit

"Let anyone who is thirsty come to me and drink. Whoever believes in me, as Scripture has said, rivers of living water will flow from within them. By this he meant the Spirit, whom those who believed in him were later to receive." ( John 7:37-39a).

Just imagine what an amazing grace it is that God with his own presence wants to dwell in us through his Holy Spirit ( John 14:16-17). On a visit to Jerusalem during the Feast of Tabernacles, Jesus promised that he would give the Holy Spirit as rivers of living water. God wants us to be overflowing with

His Spirit and His life. But, how filled with the Holy Spirit can we become? I have met many who have experienced the presence of God and have literally overflowed with joy and life. They have laughed, cried, prayed and spoken in other tongues. Even so, sometime I have realized that beneath the surface of bubbling joy there are still a few things that they need to deal with. In other words, one can be filled with the Spirit without being completely filled by the Spirit. Does that sound strange? Let me give you an example. If you start to fill a pan with water, sooner or later the water in the pan will overflow. Is the pan then full of water or not? The answer to this question depends on whether there is anything else in the pan besides the water. Let's assume that before you started adding water, you had put some potatoes in the pot. In that case, the pan isn't completely filled with water, even if it overflows. Instead, it is filled with both water and potatoes. In a similar way, God can fill us with His Spirit and we can find ourselves overflowing and functioning in the gifts and power of the Spirit. But the truth is that we all have a whole bunch of potatoes taking up space in our lives. It can be sin, selfish ambitions, fear, worry, lust, doubt or other baggage that takes up space in the pots and pans of life. God longs to rid us of our potatoes so that His presence can fill us even more. We can function in the gifts of the Spirit even if there are some potatoes in the way, but the fruit of the Spirit becomes increasingly visible when the potatoes start to disappear as we are being sanctified. Walking with Jesus, we need to be on our guard and constantly be aware of any potatoes that may be taking space from God in our lives. As we walk further along the way of salvation, this is one of the things that we will need to deal with. The more space God gets in our lives, the more of his love, power and strength we can be a bearers of. This is an important part of our journey. God wants rivers of living water to flow from within us so He can overflow to others. When God calls us to walk our lives in fellowship with Him, it is to a life where He wants us to be completely filled with His love and presence. For us, that means, a life containing fewer of our own potatoes.

# PART 3

## KEEP ON GOING

In the last part of this book, we will discover together
how God can lead us along paths where our faith
deepens, grows, and bears fruit.

Walking with Jesus is not a journey along a broad,
straight road, but rather a daily walk on a narrow path
as we keep in step with the Holy Spirit.
Sometimes the road leads through joy, hardship, peace,
suffering, and sorrow. But God has promised to guide
all those who seek Him, so that we may walk in His
good and perfect will.

# Chapter 9

## FURTHER ON THE WAY TO SALVATION!

"He must become greater; I must become less."
John 3:30

Several years ago, I read Rick Warren's book *A Purpose driven life*. I was deeply shaken when I read the first chapter and the words "It's not about you!". I felt really provoked, and at the same time I experienced an enormous sense of liberation. God was not created to exist for me, to meet my longings and my needs. God is the one who created the world. "For from him and through him and for him are all things. To him be the glory forever! Amen." (Romans 11:36) We owe our existence to the purposes of God. As we walk with Jesus, our goal should be to let our lives be more and more about Him. Traditionally, we have used the word *sanctification* to describe the transformation that we go through as our lives become increasingly more Christlike. Another way to describe sanctification is with the words that John the Baptist used, "He must become greater; I must become less" ( John 3:30). Or to put it even more bluntly: It's all about Him. Walking on the road of salvation is a journey, where we are called to repent, be transformed and renewed, where Jesus is at the center of our lives. For this transformation to take place, we need to let our thoughts be renewed and that begins to happen when our worldview changes from believing that life ultimately is about us to believing that life is ultimately about Him. This is perhaps the most important and fundamental insight that a person ever can have, but at the same time it is a shattering realization that will dramatically turn our lives upside down. If we are to be honest, we have to admit that we live, for the most part, for our own purposes and give our time to the small world that is close at hand. When we realize who God is, we begin to understand why we exist in the first place, making our own little world so much bigger. God is not someone in a galaxy far far away, but he is at the center of everything that exists. The Bible gives us the wonderful insight that God is the origin of all things. We cannot live life apart from him and at the same time fulfill the purpose of being human. The word of God, the Bible, tells us the real truth about ourselves and the world we live in. The Bible helps us see to the world as it really is, that it is God's handiwork and that "through him and for him are all things" (Romans 11:36). As John writes in the introduction to his gospel: "without him nothing was made that has been made" ( John 1:3).

### Honesty leads the way

If God's intention is to shape us in the image his son (Romans 8:28), we need to reflect on what it is that can make that change. I have to be honest and admit that I still have a long way to go. Maybe you think that the pastor is a little holier than everyone else, in that case you should talk to my wife or my children. There are so many potatoes (see page 112-113) in my life that make me fall. For example, I am forgetful, impulsive and often impatient, especially when it comes to my family. However, I can be patient with puzzles, sermons, a congregation and people that I don't really know. Unfortunately, I often hurt my family when they see my worst sides, my tired, unfocused, and neglectful side. For me, it's easy to find excuses and say, "That's just the way I am" or "I try, but I just can't do any better." Sometimes I wish my wife would just accept me as I am, but she loves me too much to do that. It is the same with God. He loves us too much to let us carry around all these "potatoes" in our lives. He also wants to help us when we stray and get lost on paths that take us away from Him. Paul writes, "the gospel… is the power of God that brings salvation to everyone who believes" (Romans 1:16). The gospel, the good news of Jesus, in not only a power that makes us righteous as we are born again, it is also a power that can sanctify us so that we become more and more like Jesus. I like to use the word sanctification as I think that it captures the essence of this transformation. God can change our flaws and bad attitudes as we allow ourselves to be transformed by Him and, step by step, be renewed to bear more and more of God's holy character within us. When Paul writes to the church in Galatia, he give a crystal-clear description of the work that the Holy Spirit wants to do in us. He wants to give us love, joy, peace, forbearance, kindness, goodness, faithfulness, gentleness, and self-control (Galathians 5:22–23). These nine flavors that we previously have talked about, are really put to test mainly in our close relationships, especially within our own families. Anyone can go to church on a Sunday, pray the right prayers, say the right words, and be patient with strangers. But it is always so much harder to be patient with those who are closest to us, since it is they who really seem to get on our nerves. It is not difficult to memorize Bible verses and stand in front of others to give a testimony, but to love those who hurt us is really difficult. It is precisely this struggle that we find ourselves in as children of God, a struggle that Paul described when he said in Romans 7 that "For I do not do the good I want to do, but the evil I do not want to do - this I keep on doing", before adding "Who will rescue me from this body that is subject to death?" (Romans 7:19, 24) What he asks is "Who will deliver me from the influence of sin, who can sanctify me and who can pluck the potatoes out of my life so that I can be completely filled with the Spirit of God?"

A few years ago I had a conversation with a member in the church that I served, suddenly the person asked: "What good use do I have of God?" I know it was an honestly question, but really it was the wrong question. If God exists and, if he has created us, the right question must be: "What good use does God have of me?" For many of us, it can be both a foreign and a frightening question. What if God were to paint a picture of a different life than the one that I had planned for myself? The idea that the goal of life is for us to be useful to God may run counter to the image of God as our friend and companion. But even if that might be a new way of thinking to you, it is certainly not a new idea to the writers of the Bible. It is only when we walk with God, that we discover what it truly means to be alive. Being sanctified means that the new thoughts of repentance, faith, baptism and the life of the Spirit become increasingly more present in and through us. Life should be about God, because without Him there is no life. The great evangelist Billy Graham summed up this truth in these words: "We should not pray for God to be on our side but pray that we may be on God's side." This means that we should not ask God to walk with us along the path that we have chosen, instead we should ask him for the grace to walk on the path that He has chosen. This is where we find peace and meaning, and where, through the process of sanctification, life becomes less about us and more about Him.

It is when we abide in Christ through prayer that we open the door so that this transformation and sanctification can take place. At best, it is only with limited success that we can force ourselves to do better. Only God can perform the miracle to transform us from the inside. When we remain or abide in Jesus we give God the opportunity to bring forth fruit in our life. Through reading the Bible and prayer we connect with God's own heart and give Him both the time and space to shape us through His word and His Holy Spirit. There is a deep devine mystery that happens when we remain in Christ and in his word ( John 15:1-10). As disciples, prioritizing and setting aside fixed times for prayer and reding His word has tremendous results for our walk with Christ. Why not ask God to help you discover what He wants to do in and through your life, then write those thoughts down and pray over them persistently and with perseverance. You will be surprised at what a prayer of faith, can accomplish in the kingdom of God and in our lives. He "is able to do immeasurably more than all we ask or imagine" (Ephesians 3:20). The prayer of the apostles shook the prison so that their shackles fell off; their prayers healed the sick and took them far away from their home in Galilee. Prayer has always paved the way for the impossible, tearing down obstacles that seemed insurmountable and opened doors to the unimaginable. When we pray with perseverance for what is on God's heart, we will be living the kind of life where God becomes greater and more real. Bold prayers honor God, because it is only when we have complete trust in Him that He can show His greatness. At the same time, God honors bold prayers, he loves to answer when we ask him for the impossible. The big question is: who is at the center of our prayers, is it God or is it Me?

## Cat or Dog?

Once in conversation with my friend Jonas, he claimed that people are often formed by a cat theology rather than a dog theology. He saw my questioning look and quickly explained his reasoning. When an owner of a dog gives the dog a treat, the dog thinks "my owner is so kind to me, they are so wonderful". But, when the owner of a cat gives the cat a treat the cat thinks "My owner is so kind to me, they must think I am so wonderful." Immediately I understood what Jonas meant. Several times since then, this way of thinking has come to mind, and I have used it in my teaching. The sad truth is, that many of us come to God with the attitude that God is there for us, because we are so wonderful. I dare say that we in the Western world have created a theology that is according to cats, where God exists for us and to meet our desires. We seek a God who will meet our needs, fulfill our dreams, and help us reach our full potential, because after all, we are so wonderful. To be honest, there is some truth in this. God really does see us as His beloved sons and daughters, and He wants the best for us. But in the long run, this way of thinking is destructive, as everything, including God, revolves around me, myself, and I. Humankind may be the crown of God's creation, but we are far from the center of it.

The cat's progress in the arena of faith has, during the last century, programmed us to believe that we are the center of everything. During the Middle Ages, people were so ignorant that they believed the sun, the moon, and all the stars circled around the earth. Today, we have come much further in our understanding of the universe, so far, in fact, that we now know with certainty that everything, including God, revolves around *me*. We have emphasized words like independence and self-reliance, arguing that we must follow our own dreams and be true to ourselves in order to reach our full potential in order for us to be happy. But it is ironic that, despite spending so much time finding ourselves and following our hearts, we have never been more lost. This lostness makes us feel like failures, insignificant and lonely. Sometimes I wonder if we think of God as the missing piece in the big jigsaw puzzle of life, the piece that will complete the puzzle and make our lives better. I love doing those 1000 pieces puzzles, but when it comes to our life's, we need to realize that God is not just another piece we need to fit into our lives to make us whole. If life doesn't turn out as we hoped, or if we don't become successful and happy, our "cat's theology" will logically conclude that God was not the missing piece after all. Instead of seeing God as just a piece of the puzzle, we should see Him as the table on which we place all the different pieces of life's grand jigsaw. A repentant mind and sanctified thoughts help us realize that our life is all about Him, because, after all, He is so wonderful.

Our cats also sneak into our churches, and if we are honest, we like our church to be accepted by the world and society. In order to achieve this, we tend to exclude any ideas or beliefs that those outside the church might criticize. We want a faith that is safe, accepted, and private. The problem is that many times we do exactly what Paul warned us not to do: namely, conform to this world (Romans 12:2). By doing so, we are no longer the salt and light of the world that Jesus wants us to be (Matthew 5:13). But if everything is created through Him and for Him, we must ask ourselves the biggest and most important question of all: What does God want? What is His will and His plan for His creation? God's answer might be something completely different from our plans or our dreams.

There is a book in the Old Testament called Ecclesiastes, written by King Solomon. Solomon, who the Bible considers to be the wisest man who ever lived (1 Kings 3:12), paints a rather bleak picture of humankind as we are in constant pursuit of wealth and happiness. Time and time again, he used the strange phrase, namely "a chasing after the wind" (Ecclesiastes 1:14). It's a rather strange saying, because we can't chase after the wind, let alone catch it, but that's exactly what he's referring to. If we chase after earthly things like wealth, affirmation, and happiness, we will ultimately have nothing to show for it. Our hands will be empty the day we meet our creator and that is precisely why God himself invites us to live a better life where we are a part of His great plan for His world. By seeking God's will, we can, during our short years here on earth, lay up treasure in eternity (1 Timothy 6:19), a treasure that can never be destroyed (Matthew 6:20). This is what Paul experienced and what he wanted to convey to his disciple Timothy. Paul encouraged his young associate to be bold when he says:

"Command those who are rich in this present world not to be arrogant nor to put their hope in wealth, which is so uncertain, but to put their hope in God, who richly provides us with everything for our enjoyment. Command them to do good, to be rich in good deeds, and to be generous and willing to share. In this way they will lay up treasure for themselves as a firm foundation for the coming age, so that they may take hold of the life that is truly life" (1 Timothy 6:17-19).

This is true, and like Salomon we can say: "Stop chasing after the wind."

As we are being sanctified, we learn to walk on the path of salvation where sin loses, bit by bit, its grip on us. God becomes greater, we become less. This is the beginning of our journey and is of great importance for how our continued walk with Jesus will be. It is when repentance, faith, baptism and the Holy Spirit are the foundation on which we stand that we are best equipped to walk further on with Jesus. When we listen to older, fellow travelers, a common theme seems to be that life with Jesus hasn't always been easy. They will tell you that there were days when they didn't see where they were going, and when God seemed to be nowhere to be found. At those times it is encouraging to remember that the Bible was not written by people who were strangers to suffering, trials and temptations. We can see that their faith carried them through trouble, even when, humanly speaking, there were many good reasons for them to give up. They clung on to God because they realized that: He is so wonderful and that life is not about them, but all about Him. After all, without God, we are forever lost, but with Him we are well on the way to salvation.

# Chapter 10

## MATURING AND GROWING IN FAITH

"But blessed is the one who trusts in the Lord, whose confidence is in him. They will be like a tree planted by the water that sends out its roots by the stream. It does not fear when heat comes; its leaves are always green. It has no worries in a year of drought and never fails to bear fruit."

Jeremiah 17:7-8

When we have walked for a while on the road with Jesus, sooner or later, we will come to a point where God wants to test our faith in order to deepen our trust in Him. Since faith is not primarily about believing in God's existence but rather trusting in Him, God will lead us step by step down paths where our faith and trust can deepen and become even stronger. Often, this can be on roads that lead us through wastelands and paths of trials. In the Middle East, the alternations between rain and drought give an olive tree its strength. A tree with a rich supply of water in its soil will, to a larger extent, have roots that are shallow. Therefore, it is during the dry years when the water is found deeper down that the tree is forced to make its roots grow deeper. It is the rain that gives the tree its life, but it is the dry years that make it strong and durable. The result is that, over time, an olive tree that has experienced hard times and drought can bear more fruit and give richer harvests than a tree that hasn't. It is the same with us. We need dry years and times in the desert for the roots of faith and trust to penetrate deeper into the ground. If everything always goes our way, we will have no need to dig or let our roots go deeper. Here arises an important question: What do we do when the walk of faith on the way to salvation leads us out into that dry wasteland?

We all want healthy, green leaves and branches that bear fruit, but we won't see that unless we let our roots grow deeper during times of drought and seasons in the wilderness. Many of the writers of the Bible had this very experience. Take Habakkuk for example. He cried out to the Lord and wondered where God was, because evil seemed to be spreading among His chosen people. God's answer shocked Habakkuk to his core. God's solution to the evil among the Jews was that He was going to allow an even more evil people to invade them. Where's the logic in that? Sometimes God can allow us to go through trials and hardship in order to shape and transform us so that we will be of greater use to Him. God's great plan is to save the whole earth, and we are the tools He uses to reach this lost world and bring people back to God. God almost always chooses people to do His will and fulfill His plans, and that is ultimately why He created us in the first place. He wants to sharpen and reshape us, and to accomplish that, He sometimes allows us to face difficulties and setbacks.

Right after Jesus was baptized and filled with the Spirit he was led into the wilderness to be tempted (Matthew 4:1-11). After 40 days of fasting and prayer, the devil came to and questioned Jesus' identity, his calling and his character. Time and again Jesus responded to the devil's accusations with the words "it is written" (Luke 4:4, 8, 10). When the devil wants to get to us,

God's word is always the weapon that we should use to fight him off. And if you have read the passage you probably have noticed that even the devil quoted scriptures in order to tempt Jesus (Luke 4:9-11). This way of corrupting God's word is Satan's oldest trick. In the garden of Eden he questioned God's own word by saying: "Did God really say" (Genesis 3:1). This spiritual battle that Jesus Himself faced is much more real than we often think, and it is a crucial part of our walk in the wilderness.

## A spiritual reality

Although trials, difficulties, and droughts are a natural part of our walk with Jesus, the spiritual battle is a dimension that we sometimes tend to neglect. "Your enemy the devil prowls around like a roaring lion looking for someone to devour" (1 Peter 5:8). He is also described as the one who, with his crafty attacks, wants to lure us away from the path of salvation so that we cannot stand firm in the faith (Ephesians 6:10–18). As a teenager I read a couple of extremely exciting books written by Frank E. Peretti. Even though I am a slow reader, I managed to quickly read through both *This Present Darkness* and *Piercing the Darkness*. In these novels, we see strange things happening in the small town of Ashton in the USA. We discover that these events are connected to what is happening at the same time in the unseen spiritual world, where angels, demons, and the prayers of believers play a major role in how the story unfolds. These fictional accounts may not be entirely theologically accurate in their descriptions of the spiritual realm, but they were nonetheless tremendously thrilling to read.

These books had two effects on me, one positive and one not so positive. On the negative side, they stirred up fear in me. In both books, demons were portrayed as having more power than they actually do, and everything seemed to depend on our ability to pray. On the positive side, they opened my eyes to the reality of the spiritual realm, even for us here in Sweden, where I live. But they also awakened in me a longing for prayer and a deeper desire to seek God's kingdom. When Paul in his letter to the Ephesians writes about this spiritual realm, he does so with the words:

> "For our struggle is not against flesh and blood, but against the rulers, against the authorities, against the powers of this dark world and against the spiritual forces of evil in the heavenly realms." (Ephesians 6:12)

There is a struggle that we are all called to fight, a battle that we are often too blind to see.

In our walk with God, there is so much at stake. Since there are two ways we can spend eternity, we had better make the right choices while we still have the time and opportunity to do so. In his letter to the church in Ephesus, Paul urges the believers there to

> "Be very careful, then, how you live (walk), not as unwise but as wise, making the most of every opportunity, because the days are evil. Therefore, do not be foolish, but understand what the Lord's will is." (Ephesians 5:15-17, italics mine)

To manage to walk in these evil days, we need God's wisdom to understand what His will is. If we can discern what the Lord wants, we will see that He wants to use us so that more people will come to know Jesus Christ as their Lord and Savior. We are called to invite more lost people into God's great family. And that is what the devil, first and foremost, fights against. He is a thief who "comes only to steal and kill and destroy." ( John 10:10). The devil wants to steal our peace and boldness and make us sit down on the side of life's road, arms crossed, silently watching people pass us by, wandering away from the one true path. In other countries, the devil roars like a lion to frighten and instill fear in people. However, in Sweden and the west, the devil seems to have found it most effective to put us to sleep with a lullaby. In the book *The Generous Gambler*, Baudelaire made this insightful statement: "The greatest trick the Devil ever pulled was to convince the world he didn't exist.". The devil is hard at work making us quiet and passive so that God's kingdom doesn't extend through us to other people. He wants to make us indifferent and comfortable, but first he wants to stop us praying, because prayer is the weapon by which we see God's kingdom advance. It is through prayer that we see God's will done on earth, just as it is in heaven.

I am convinced that the spiritual realm is far more real than we often realize. Angels and demons are all around us, and as God's children, we have a God-given authority in the spiritual world, an authority we've only just begun to discover. If we truly understood the power and impact of our prayers, we would be amazed by the trust God has placed in us. "And these signs will accompany those who believe", Jesus said, "In my name they will drive out demons, … they will place their hands on sick people, and they will get well." (Mark 16:17–18). Walking as a Christian is to do the will of the Father and fight against the devil and be on our guard against his sneaky attacks (Ephesians 6:11). The best way to uncover the devil's plans is to be constantly filled with God's word, live Spirit filled lives and walk closely with other believers in His church. Or as the old Chinese saying goes: "It is better to light a candle than to curse the darkness."

DAY 29

## To welcome and expect suffering and trials

"In this world you will have trouble. But take heart! I have overcome the world." ( John 16:33)

For many of us who wish to have a smooth, convenient faith, it is hard to swallow the fact that Jesus and his apostles talked so much about suffering, trials, and struggles. After all, we want a safe and peaceful faith that does not mess too much with our lives. We want to be able to live peacefully and in harmony with everyone without standing out from the crowd or drawing unnecessary attention to ourselves. We like to read verses in the Bible about God's love and care, where we see Him as our provider and protector. We memorize verses by heart such as "The Lord is my shepherd, I lack nothing" (Psalms 23:1) but it is not quite as often that we memorize verses like "But rejoice inasmuch as you participate in the sufferings of Christ, so that you may be overjoyed when his glory is revealed2 (1 Peter 4:13). This is where some might think that if we just have strong faith, we will rise above all suffering and difficulties. But Paul, who had more faith than most of us, faced more opposition and suffering than the majority of us will ever experience. And that's not even mentioning the suffering of Jesus.

The clear teaching of the Bible is that some suffering is inevitable for those who believe in Jesus. Jesus himself, as well as Peter and Paul, tell us that we will suffer, be persecuted, humiliated and hauled into court for our faith (Mark 13:9). Jesus went so far as to say that in the same way the world has hated him, the world will hate those who follow him ( John 15:18-19). Of course, we should never seek confrontation but instead seek the good of the city in which we live ( Jeremiah 29:7) and live in peace with everyone, as far as it depends on us (Romans 12:18). But in this world we are going to meet people who will try to make us leave God's narrow path and it is, to some extent, this struggle that Jesus has in mind. In many countries, persecution and hatred and, in some cases, even imprisonment and death, are part and parcel of being a Christian. Peter writes in his first letter:

> "Dear friends, do not be surprised at the fiery ordeal that has come on you to test you, as though something strange were happening to you. But rejoice inasmuch as you participate in the sufferings of Christ, so that you may be overjoyed when his glory is revealed." (1 Peter 4:12–13)

For many of us, the thought of rejoicing when going through trials, suffering or drought is a foreign one. One of my problems is that I tend to look at the suffering with a narrow time perspective. That is why Paul so clearly points to our coming salvation and says that "our light and momentary troubles are achieving for us an eternal glory that far outweighs them all" (2 Corinthians 4:17). We have a hope ahead of us, a prize to reach for and a goal to run towards. Our coming salvation is eternal and our lives here on earth momentary and they need to be lived in the light of eternity. In this way, we can better endure hardships and live life for what really matters.

We should of course be extremely grateful if we live in a democracy where freedom of religion allows us to freely practice our faith without risk of prison or death. However, there is a risk that we will take our freedom for granted. Sometimes we can even fall into the trap of adjusting our theology or our beliefs so that people or society won't think of us as weird or reject us as intolerant. God's word must be our guide and God's church is called to be "the pillar and foundation of the truth" (1 Timothy 3:15). Being a disciple of Jesus will never be fully understood or appreciated by a world turned upside down. But we are not called to be liked or accepted, we are called to follow Jesus and live in according to his will. We are called to be a light in the darkness and a salt in this world.

For many of us, the beginning of our faith journey with Jesus started out quite pleasantly. We could see the hand of God in our circumstances and feel the touch of His Spirit in us. But during times of suffering, trials, and hardship, it can seem like God withdraws His hand from us, and many times, it is exactly what He does. The reason for this is to make us seek His face rather than His hand, to seek who He is before we seek what He does.

As we walk together with Jesus we will often end up in situations and circumstances that we won't know how to handle. An expression that I, as a pastor, have used countless times in conversation with people is "Everything that happens does not have to have a meaning, but to everything that happens, God can give a meaning". God can take even the most senseless suffering and evil in this world and, in His goodness, use it for His purposes. We can be more than certain that God will never leave us to our own devices as we walk the road with Him. "And we know that in all things God works for the good of those who love him, who have been called according to his purpose" (Romans 8:28).

## I do not want to be here

DAY 30

Paul, Peter, John and several others that we can read about in the Bible often ended up in places where they did not want to be. Some were imprisoned, others were stranded after shipwrecks or deported to an island as political prisoners. If we were to find ourselves in a similar situation, there is more than likely a great risk that we would simply sit it out and wait for better times. It is incomprehensible that, in precisely in these difficult times, when they were at a places that they didn't want to be at, that they found themselves writing history. It was when Paul sat in a prison cell that he wrote several of the letters that we have today in the Bible, a book that has changed our world. When John was imprisoned on the island of Patmos, he received a vision that for 2000 years has been a source of comfort and encouragement to suffering Christians all over the world. We recognize this pattern as a common thread throughout God's Word. After arriving in the land that God had promised land God had given Abraham, he had to leave and go to Egypt. Moses had to leave the comfort of Pharaoh's court and become a shepherd in the land of Midian.

The weeping prophet Jeremiah followed God and was thrown by his own brothers into a well. Shadrach, Meshach and Abednego were hurled into the fiery flames of a burning furnace after standing up for their beliefs. And so the list goes on. The common denominator is that God was at His most active an precisely the place that they did not want to be at. When Jesus hung on the cross abandoned, alone, betrayed, denied, broken and tormented, the place that he had literally asked God, if possible, to spare him from, that the world was forever changed.

We can see God at work in this way outside of the Bible as well. He seems to be most active in our lives when we are at places where we do not want to be. I have listened to many stories of people who have described situations or circumstances in their lives where they thought it would be impossible for them to serve God. But in hindsight, they could see that this was exactly what had happened. God is often most active when we face difficulties and trials. The risk is that a faulty theology will make us believe there is something wrong if we do not experience success. Way too many people have left the walk of faith because their theology has rejected suffering and pain. But we must also be aware of a theology that make God the giver of sickness and pain. When we end up in the swamp of despond it can be difficult to get out of there. As a pastor, it is sometimes impossible to help someone realize that it is not the place or circumstances they are in, that is their problem, but rather their attitude towards that place of circumstance. As God's children, we are bearers of His presence wherever we find ourselves, whether we become slaves, end up in the belly of a fish, are thrown into the fire, crucified or find ourselves hurled into a lion's den. For a disciple, the question should never be "Where is God in this situation?", but rather "What do I do now, when I know that God is with me in this situation?". It is when life does not turn out as we had hoped, where our faith shows its real strength and depth. King David knew this well: "Even though I walk through the darkest valley, I will fear no evil, for you are with me; your rod and your staff, they comfort me" (Psalms 23:4). Trials and difficulties are not a sign of God's absence, but rather an opportunity for us to experience God's presence.

The stories in the Bible are not made up stories of success. They are stories of real people with real problems. When we go through difficulties we are in good company. Instead of asking God to take us far away from our current circumstances, we can learn to thank God for His presence in our lives, wherever we might be. One character in the Bible who portrays this perhaps better than any other happens to be one of my personal favorites.

We find the story and history of Joseph in Genesis 37-50. Joseph was hated by his brothers, sold as a slave, falsely accused, imprisoned and finally forgotten in the dungeon by the only one who could help him. Joseph was only 17 years old when he was sold as a slave and it took thirteen long years of trials and suffering before he gained his freedom and was given a position second only to Pharaoh. Thirteen years gave plenty of time for bitterness to take root. But despite everything he went through, Joseph trusted that God was with him, and it is this faith that carried him through it all. For Joseph, adversity was not proof of God's absence, but rather an opportunity to experience God's presence. That is why we can read the wonderful words that "God was with Joseph" (Genesis 39:2, 3 & 21). In spite of his circumstances and in spite of all his misery, it was Joseph's personal experience was that God was with him. After another nine years, he was finally reconciled with his family. Toward the end of his life, as he summed up everything he had been through, he told his brothers, "You intended to harm me, but God intended it for good" (Genesis 50:20). God has an amazing way of turning evil into good and even if we don't get to see it during our lifetime, for every disciple there is always a bright future and an eternal hope.

Where, then, do we turn when we face difficulties? Some of us tend to bite the bullet and look for quick fixes. The heroes of the Bible, on the other hand, are those who, instead of relying on their own strength, turned to God in prayer, they were seeking His face and His presence, rather than His hand and his works. Abraham, Moses, Joshua, Samuel, Esther, Nehemiah, Isaiah, Peter, Paul and Jesus are just some of those who relied on God when difficulties and trials came their way. They prayed persistently until they received an answer. It wasn't necessarily the answer that they were looking for, as God "is able to do immeasurably more than all we ask or imagine" (Ephesians 3:20). In times of trail, if we dare to rely on God's power, then we will see Him intervene in the way that we needed, even if it is not always in the way we wanted, or within the timeframe that we had set. God is seldom early, but He is never late.

DAY
31

## Troubles that come with a purpose

"Praise be to the God and Father of our Lord Jesus Christ, the Father of compassion and the God of all comfort, who comforts us in all our troubles, so that we can comfort those in any trouble with the comfort we ourselves receive from God." (2 Corinthians 1:3–4)

It is with these outstanding words Paul begins his second letter to the church in Corinth. What a wonderful realization that we belong to the *Father of compassion* and the *God of all comfort*. I don't know if you saw, in that text, one little word that many of us would like to replace. After all, wouldn't we prefer a God who, instead of giving us *comfort*, helps us out of all our troubles and trials. If I am being honest, I must admit to craving God's help more than His comfort when I run into trouble.

Similarly, it is no mistake that Paul speaks here of God's comfort because His lack of help seems to have had a purpose. God wants us to become people who can be of use to Him. As we embark on the path of salvation, God accompanies us and walks alongside us. If we face hardship or trials on the way, it is not always His help that we receive, but rather His comfort and support. Remember that the troubles we are talking about are the kind of suffering that is inevitable for those who believe in Jesus. God's will is not for us to be sick or in pain, but if we are, God can comfort us and walk with us. However, it is always His will to heal, even though all is not yet healed. The amazing thing is what happens to us on the way as we are comforted. We are shaped and transformed to become more capable of bearing the comfort that God Himself has given us. It is as if God shapes us through difficulties so that we, as His instruments, can give comfort and support to others. That is Paul's point in this text: "so that we can comfort those in any trouble with the comfort we ourselves receive from God" (2 Corinthians 1:4). God equips His children to be comforters and givers of hope in the midst of an evil world.

Jesus knows what we are going through and his heart bleeds for us. But there is something greater and more important than saving us from trouble, it is to sanctify us so that we become more like him. The journey of Christian faith is lined with thorny bushes and steep, difficult climbs. The way of salvation is not a wide highway but rather a narrow path where God, who is the God of all comfort, promises to walk with us. In Psalm 23, it is in the valley of the shadow of death that God comforts us with his rod and staff, and it is also the place where we come to know the Father of compassion and the God of all comfort. Therefore, we need to learn to welcome difficulties and see them as opportunities to get to know the God of all comfort, so that we in turn can comfort others. I find this to be a helpful thought, and at the same time an incomparable benefit. Imagine that our tough moments and hardest trials can be a blessing to others, that the comfort you receive from God can be a comfort to those who are going through similar situations.

I think we all have experienced that the best comforters are those people who themselves have gone through difficulties and trials and have come through them. There is something special about hearing "It is okay" from a person who, from personal experience, deeply understands what I am going through. As we learn to count on God in all things and trust in His faithfulness, we are transformed, and our faith matures to become deeper and more durable. But not only that, a person who has experienced God's comfort and presence on the difficult paths of life is an invaluable tool in God's hand.

If we want to have a deepened faith and a living relationship with God, then His Word, as well as learning to remain and abide in Christ through prayer, becomes crucial. But we also need the fellowship of believers in the church, siblings whom we allow to be a part of our everyday lives. If we do not let God speak to us through His Word or through our Christian brothers and sisters, our journey will come to a stop at the point of doubt and silence. Instead, we can instead move forward on the path of salvation where every day can bring us closer to a life with God where He gets to be greater, and we get to be less. The goal is to walk with God constantly in our thoughts. For me, the Bible and the church have been necessary to keep me on the right course. The Bible is "a lamp for my feet, a light on my path" (Psalm 119:105). And in the church, I meet others who correct me and lead me back to the right path when I go astray. We need honest friends who not only ask us "How we are doing?" and "How are things with the family?" but also hard questions like "How are you doing with Jesus?" Friends who dare to ask that question you should hold on to and never let go of, as they are God's precious gift to you.

## On the other side

When we have walked through the valley of the shadow of death or gone through troubles, something happens to us. Just like an olive tree that gets stronger during years of drought, our faith grows and deepens during the difficult times. We are no longer the same. Often, it is only in retrospect that we realize that even the most difficult paths, have done us good, and we find that we have been shaped, transformed and changed so that we are better equipped to be used in Gods kingdom. For Peter, his denial of Jesus was a turning point in his life that humbled him and brought him to a better place. King David's troubled years when he was persecuted by Saul shaped him to become the great king that he later became "And we know that in all things God works for the good of those who love him" (Romans 8:28). God knows what he is doing, he is the master of leading His children. Like the olive tree, our roots can penetrate deeper to drink from God's life-giving water, water that can sanctify and transformed us to move forward on the way to salvation.

It is during these times, when we learn to seek His face rather than His hands, that we reach the very heart of the Christian faith. We are not merely called to believe in Him; we are called to believe, to trust, to seek His face, to abide in Him, and to remain in Him. It is often after we come out on the other side of a drought or a time in the wilderness that our faith grows stronger. This is what God longs for, that we come to know Him more deeply: who He is and what He is like. That is when we move from saying, "The Lord is our Shepherd," to declaring, "The Lord is *my* Shepherd" (Psalm 23:1), "The Lord is *my* rock" (Psalm 18:2), or, in the words of the disciple Thomas, "*My* Lord and *my* God" (John 20:28). For countless people, it has been their experience that during difficult seasons in life, God becomes personal, as we see His face, and not only the works of His hands.

# Chapter 11

## WALKING WITH JESUS IS NOT A PRIVATE MATTER

"Everybody who belongs to Christ,
belongs to everybody who belongs to Christ."
/ Stanley Jones

There's one rule for mountain hikers that we'd be foolish not to abide by: never venture out into the mountains on Your own. When we are alone on a long hike, we quickly realize that, on your own, we are not strong, but we are extremely vulnerable if something were to happen to us. Therefore, it amazes me how often Christians want to walk the path of faith on their own without any traveling companions. Perhaps they believe that their relationship with God is their own, private matter. But the Christian faith, although personal, is far from private. It is only when it is lived out with others that it can grow and mature. The Christian walk is not a solo act but rather a team sport. Being a Christian without being part of a church is like being a football player without a team or like a tuba player without an orchestra. But the most clear and biblical image that we have is that of being a child without a family. The call to Christ, is a call to his church. Stanley Jones wisely said, "Everybody who belongs to Christ belongs to everybody who belongs to Christ." As believers in Christ, we are united with each other, and we are part of the same family. Just as the Father and the Son are one,

Jesus says we are to be one with each other ( John 17:11). In other words, it is not about me and God, rather it is about God, me and His very large family.

Paul exhorts the church in Ephesus to be "rooted and established in love" so that they "may have power, *together* with all the Lord's holy people, to grasp how wide and long and high and deep is the love of Christ, and to know this love that surpasses knowledge - that you may be filled to the measure of all the fullness of God." (Ephesians 3:17–19, italics mine). Since God is by His very nature a community, a unity of Father, Son and Holy Spirit, it is only in community with all His people that we begin to really understand His fullness.

This is a mind-blowing text and shows us that the most amazing gift God gives us on our journey is fellow travelers. They are our siblings, with different backgrounds and experiences, and they can come from different parts of the world. It is only together with God's people that we can understand the width, length, height, and depth of His greatness. The church is the place where we not only meet people who are like us, but also people who are completely different from us. It is in the diversity we encounter in God's church that we find ourselves stretched, challenged, enriched, and blessed.

Immanuel Church in Malmö, where I serve, is a church with members from about twenty different nationalities. About forty percent of the church members come from a culture other than the Swedish one. There are professionals, company managers, nurses, workers without papers, schoolteachers, and so on. In our church community, we have both former alcoholics and those who have never even tasted a drop of alcohol. There are singles, widows, divorcees and couples who have celebrated their golden anniversary. There are young, older, short, tall, introverts and extroverts. In other words, we are a blissful mix of many different kinds of people. What unites us is not our backgrounds, our interests, or our culture, but that we all proclaim Jesus as Lord and, therefore, as children of the living God, brothers and sisters. I am well aware that the church is far from perfect; it is fragile, vulnerable, and full of problems. But when it is working well, there is nothing more powerful or beautiful on earth. Whatever we may think of the church or each other, God loves His family above all else.

The church is God's answer to the question "How will the world find out what Jesus has done on the cross?" It is the fellowship of Jesus' believers that is called to spread the good news of the kingdom of God wherever it goes. When Jesus spoke of God's church, he says that he will build it and that not even the gates of hell will overcome it (Mathew 16:18). The word Matthew uses for "church" is *ecclesia* which simply means "a gathering of people". The mandate that Jesus gave to his church is unimaginably great.

Moreover, the church is the ultimate tool that God uses to make known to the rulers and authorities in the heavenly realms, the manifold wisdom of God (Ephesians 3:10). The devil hates the church and does everything he can to split, divide and create confusion in God's family. Every time a believer says that they can manage on their own without help from others in God's family, is a victory for the devil. God's desire is that together in the fellowship of His church we should be able to understand His greatness and show the world what Christ, His Messiah, has done. Therefore, there is a struggle in the spiritual realm, not only over our faith but also over our unity and life in God's *ecclesia*, His gathering of people. Every time the kingdom of God advances in power with healing, deliverance and reconciliation, with people becoming God's children and joining His family, it happens at the expense of the devil. Together, with our fellow travelers on God's road to salvation, we are called to fight the good fight. The evangelist Reinhard Bonke coined the expression "Let us plunder hell and populate heaven." This describes our mission very well. As God's people, we need to realize that together in community, our common purpose is to lead people on to the path of salvation and then help each other to follow Jesus in everything.

DAY
33

## One body with many parts

When Paul writes to the church in Ephesus, he says that we 2are no longer foreigners and strangers, but *fellow citizens* with God's people and also members of His household" (Ephesians 2:19 italics mine). This means that people who would normally be strangers to each other, can in the church, become God's household and His dwelling place. Together we are so much more than we ever could be on our own. The church has often been good at emphasizing "Jesus in me" and that "I am a child of God", but what Paul highlights here is the unity and togetherness. Furthermore, he writes that we are "built on the foundation of the apostles and prophets, with Christ Jesus himself as the chief cornerstone" (Ephesians 2:20). Then he states that through Jesus we "are being built *together* to become a dwelling in which God lives by his Spirit" (Ephesians 2:22 italics mine). In other words, God not only lives through His

Spirit in individuals but also in His church. When we gather together as church we do so as "holy temple in the Lord… a dwelling in which God lives" (Ephesians 2:21-22). Each of us is a building block that God is using to build His church in this world. And this is exactly what Jesus also told his disciples when they went to Caesarea Philippi. Jesus there promised that he would build his church (Matthew 16:18). We who used to be guests and strangers are now the very family that He wants to live in. It is therefore only when we become a part of God's church that we can fully live out His perfect will and plan for our lives. It is true that the Spirit of God dwells in each one of us personally, but the fullness of God dwells in the church (Ephesians 3:19) and as I previously wrote, His plan is that "through the church, the manifold wisdom of God should be made known to the rulers and authorities in the heavenly realms (Ephesians 3:10).

Before Paul became a disciple of Jesus he was persecuting his followers and had received permission from the Sanhedrin, the Jewish leaders in Jerusalem, to go to Damascus and throw the Christian believers into prison. As he made his way there "suddenly a light from heaven flashed around him. He fell to the ground and heard a voice say to him, "Saul, Saul, why do you persecute me?" "Who are you, Lord?" Saul asked. "I am Jesus, whom you are persecuting" (Acts 9:1-5). Saul could have argued that he was not persecuting Jesus at all but the believers. Perhaps it was there in the dust that Paul's theology of the body was born. He realized that Jesus equates the church with himself. Speak harshly of the church and you speak harshly of Jesus, love the church and you love Jesus, withdraw from the church and you withdraw from Jesus. This same image then recurs time and again throughout Paul's letters and has given us a greater understanding of what it means for us to be *church*. Together, says Paul, we form different parts of Jesus' body here on earth. Paul connects us together and says "If one part suffers, every part suffers with it; if one part is honored, every part rejoices with it" (1 Corinthians 12:26). This is an experience we all know only to well. Remember how it feels when you stub your little toe on the coffee table. If one part suffers, the whole body suffers and we cry out in pain. The solution, then, is not amputation but rather care, rest and recovery. Therefore, we must be a community where the struggling, doubting, sick and wounded can find healing as they are embraced by the care of God's family.

What if we understood what a help we could be to one another if we allowed our brothers and sisters in Christ to speak hard truths to guide us? If we recognize our need for honest friends like this, then God can do amazing things in us. In his first letter from prison to the Christian believers in Philippi, Paul urges them to "continue to work out your salvation with fear and trembling" (Philippians 2:12). This collective call is written in the plural, not to individuals, but rather to the entire congregation, that we, together as His church, would work out our salvation. Give that some thought!

I remember a story of a young man who visits an elderly mentor. The young man shared how much he had struggled with his faith as he tried to live as Jesus' disciple. But he had stopped going to church and was now ready to stop believing in God altogether. As the young man spoke the elderly mentor sat looking at the fire burning in the fireplace. The young man asked, "So what should I do? What's wrong with me? How did

I end up here? Why is God so quiet?". Without a word, the elderly man walked over to the fireplace, plucked out a burning log and placed it on beside the fire. Within a minute or so the fire had gone out and all that could be seen were a few thin wisps of smoke rising from the log. The elderly man rose again and put the now extinguished log back into the fire and immediately it caught fire again. Without a word being spoken, the message couldn't have been any clearer. On our own the fire in us will soon dwindle, but when we share our faith with others then it will burn more brightly and more intensely. There are far too many people that have walked away from friends and church when they done best in leaning on the support of the church and allowed themselves to be guided and helped by their brothers and sisters in God's family. We need to constantly remind each other that we need wise travel companions to journey with us on the road to salvation. This is something that God realizes and that is why He has given us his own family to walk with.

In 2024, I was involved in a large Christian conference. Rachel Turner was preaching about the importance of every part of the church body functioning as it should. She said that in order for us to be a church where every generation feels loved, valued, and important, we all need to get involved in investing in the next generation. This young generation is leaving the church at an alarming rate because the church body is not working as God intended. After she had finished speaking, there was a time of prayer and ministry. I felt God say that there was someone in that big barn who had an injured left shoulder as the result of an accident. This I then shared with those present. At the end of the meeting approached me and asked if I could pray for a woman with an injured left shoulder. I asked my colleague Kim to join me and so we prayed. I placed my hand on the woman's left shoulder and said, "Thank you, Jesus, that through your wounds, she is now healed!" I did not have time to pray any longer before she asked, "What is happening to me?" She slowly started to move her fingers and then her arm and so I asked her "Does it still hurt?" She looked up at me and answered, "It's not that!" Since everyone around her was far happier about what was happening than I was I asked them to explain. She told me that, five years ago, she had fallen so badly in a public bathing house that she had torn the nerves in her shoulder, causing her whole arm to be almost completely paralyzed. She had visited several neurologists who all told her that there was nothing that could be done. For five years she had been handling her pain with strong painkillers and her shoulder had been put in a special cast. In front of our eyes, she removed the cast and starting to move her arm around. Her seven years old son was crying and didn't understand what was happening with his mum as she, for the first time since he was a baby, lifted him up and hugged him with both her arms. I realized there and then that we had just seen Rachels sermon play out before our very eyes. When the whole body is fully functioning properly we can embrace the next generation. There is nothing like the local church when it is working right. We need each other and together we can be the church that God can use to reach the next generation as well as the whole earth. And on top of that we really need to step out in the authority and the life in the power of the holy spirit. God want us as a church to see His kingdom come and His will be done on earth as it is in heaven (Mathew 6:10). The Spirit always wants to manifest himself in each one of us for the common good as he distributes his gifts to each one, just as he determines. (1 Corinthians 12:7-11).

## A growing faith together

As a gathering of disciples, we can't be satisfied with sitting in rows looking at the back of each other's necks. We need to find ways to sit in circles and look into each other's eyes. There is an enormous strength in being in a small group of Christian brothers and sisters with whom we regularly meet and share life together. These small groups are often the key to be a church characterized by discipleship, care and the warmth of community.

Outside the life and warmth of the church, faith can quickly cool and love for Jesus start to burn less brightly. Church then tends to become something that we *should* go to and *ought to attend.* That is why it is so important to constantly return to what God has to says about His family. God's church, in all its brokenness, is His answer to people's loneliness, weakness, worry and longing for deeper meaning and purpose in life. The church is supposed to help people go from being eternally lost to finding their way back home to God again.

## Clean or dirty hands?

DAY
34

One thing constantly frustrates me. Some Christians seem to believe that a pure and holy life must be lived in isolation from everything that they consider sinful. That is the exact same idea that the Pharisees had about sanctification. They thought that they had to live far away from anything and anyone that could taint them. This led them to create a system where they never had to associate with people who did not measure up to their high standard. Their philosophy was, "clean hands leads to clean hearts", but when Jesus stepped into the world he showed them a completely different way to live a holy life. His way of living was the perfect example of how someone with a pure and holy heart shouldn't be afraid to get their hands dirty. That is why he touched the lepers and the sick, took time to talk with a Samaritan woman and even drank water from her jar, and to everyone's surprise he invited himself to feast at the homes of sinners. "When he saw the crowds, he had compassion on them, because they were harassed and helpless, like sheep without a shepherd (Matthew 9:36) and the very reason that he came to earth was "to seek and to save the lost" (Luke 19:10). Jesus is the ultimate model for how we should live our lives, and therefore, we must never be so busy keeping our hands clean that we end up with dirty hearts. God's church must, just like Jesus, be pure in heart and never be afraid to get our hands dirty. Nor should we be afraid to invite those who are lost and helpless to join us. A clean heart should make us want to get our hands dirty.

## De-greecing the church

When the Christian faith first emerged, it was primarily in a Jewish context, but pretty soon the good news of Jesus spread far and wide. As the gospel message reached beyond the borders of Israel to Greece the gnostic worldview quickly left its greasy fingerprints on the church of God. The ancient Greeks had divided reality into the material and spiritual realms, the spiritual being better and superior to the material which was for the uneducated and the simple.

They taught that the human body belongs to the worldly realm and as such was separated from the spiritual realm. As early as the first century, this gnostic worldview began to seep into the church, leading its members to question Jesus' dual nature: surely, he can't be God (spiritual) if he at the same time is human (material)?

The result was that they downplayed Jesus' humanity, producing such texts as the Gospel of Thomas where Jesus is given divine powers even as a child. In some other texts, Jesus' divinity was belittled as they struggled to believe that Jesus the man could also be God. But God has never separated the spiritual from the physical. Whether we eat, drink, work or sleep, it is connected with our spiritual life with God. What we do with our body has consequences for our life with God. Therefore, there are no secular, worldly jobs. All jobs, from God's point of view, must be done to glorify Him, whether we drive a bus, take care of children, study, preach sermons or work in a warehouse. We must never categorize our deeds into spiritual or worldly. God connects everything together and all is part of the same reality. "So whether you eat or drink or whatever you do, do it all for the glory of God" (1 Corinthians 10:31). We still find this ancient Greek way of thinking in our churches. We think the worship leader has a more spiritual role than the sound engineer. This way of thinking leads us to look down on each other, and in the worst case can cause the church to become pharisaical, shutting out the very people we should be trying to reach so that they don't make us dirty. It is high time that we de-greeced the church.

As Jesus calls us to be sanctified, we must, like him, be willing to get our hands dirty. We must not isolate ourselves from the world but instead step out in the world with him and desire to share the grace, forgiveness and comfort that we ourselves have received from Him. God never intended holiness as a way for us to isolate ourselves from the world, but rather as a way for us to function in the world. God has blessed me with a wise wife, and she has a special expression for how we, as God's church, should see ourselves. She says, "We must see ourselves as a people who are different."

There has to be something different about us and how we live, how we choose to manage our money, our time or our sexuality according to God's principles and commands. This may lead others to see us as odd, but we must have the courage to be different, a people of God whose priority is to follow Jesus, come what may. We are to love those whom the world rejects, speak the truth in the face of lies and spread the kingdom of God in the midst of a world that has turned its beck on Him. And whatever we do, we should do it to the glory of God (1 Corinthians 10:31)

John Burke wrote a book entitled *"Come as You Are"*. It's a really good book, but its title can easily be misunderstood. Of course, we want everyone to come to church, and of course, everyone can come exactly as they are. The goal, however, is not for them to simply join a church but for them to experience the transformation that can only be found in the gospel. Our message should be "Come as you are but become like Jesus". God's will is that we become "conformed to the image of his Son, that he might be the firstborn among many brothers and sisters." (Romans 8:29). Our faith in Jesus can and should change the way we live, but this is not something that will happen automatically. We need to actively choose the right path and allow God to transform us, through his word, in his presence, and together with his family.

## The narrow road

To walk in the light of His life is a daily decision, to pick up our cross and follow Him (Luke 9:23). At the same time, it is a life where all of us who are weary and burdened can find rest in Jesus. We can take His yoke upon us and learn from Him, who is gentle and humble in heart. In doing so, we will find rest for our souls (Matthew 11:28–29). To follow Christ in this world is to live with God's new thoughts, or in the words of Paul, to let our minds be renewed so that we can discern what God's good and perfect will is (Romans 12:2). But reaching that place doesn't happen overnight or through a quick ministry time at church. Walking in renewal is a journey with the Holy Spirit, where we keep in step with Him (Galatians 5:25).

Jesus said that we will bear fruit if we remain in Him ( John 15:5). Pastor and author John Mark Comer describes the Christian walk as an apprenticeship: learning to be with Jesus in order to become like Jesus, so that we can do what Jesus did. Our Heavenly Father desires that we be filled with His Spirit, so that we may become like His Son, as we are being transformed into His image (2 Corinthians 3:18). As His beloved sons and daughters, our goal should be to be useful in His hand as He completes His great divine plan, until Jesus Christ, the King of Glory, returns to this broken world and makes it brand new.

After three decades as a pastor, I must admit that I haven't always succeeded in leading people to the place where they are truly transformed into Christlikeness. I have led many on the road of salvation, teaching about repentance, faith, baptism, and the Holy Spirit. I have urged Christians to read their Bibles and to pray. I have witnessed God's amazing grace transform lives despite my own flaws and limited leadership. I've had the privilege of seeing many find a deep, enduring faith, walking firmly with Jesus. But at other times, I've only been able to lead people part of the way. There is a path for every believer to walk, much of what I've written about in this book. But how do we help people move beyond those first steps in faith and grow into lives filled with love, joy, peace, patience, kindness, and so on? I must admit that my focus has often been on *adding* to already busy lives. We add church, small group, Bible reading, prayer, and serving. But I haven't been as good at helping disciples learn to *subtract*. When we only add, life becomes messy, crowded, and hurried. In his book *The Ruthless Elimination of Hurry*, John Mark Comer writes: "Here's my point: the solution to an overbusy life is not more time. It's to slow down and simplify our lives around what really matters." And if you were to ask Jesus what truly matters, He would say: *"Love the Lord your God with all your heart and with all your soul and with all your mind."* And in the same breath, He would add: *"Love your neighbor as yourself."* (Matthew 22:37-39). This outpouring of love, toward God and others, is the fruit of being with Jesus. It is His presence that brings about true transformation in our lives, as the Holy Spirit cultivates His sweet fruit within us.

## A love like mashed potato's

In my teens I came across an incredible book called *Disciple*. Juan Carlos Ortiz describes in a stunning way how God touched a church in Argentina. The book is packed with images and parables that shed light on one thing after another. I still remember how Juan Carlos likened the community of disciples to potatoes. He wrote that first we are potatoes on a plant or family, and then, after we come to faith, we are gathered up into one and the same sack. In the sack we rub up against each other and feel the closeness to the other potatoes, but we are still separated potatoes. If we get closer to each other, we might peel each other's skin and suddenly they'll be nothing between us. This is a true community, but we can still differ between what is *mine* from what is *yours*. Finally, God's Spirit mashes us together with his love. We become mashed potatoes, and no one considers anything his own anymore, but we share everything we have with each other (Acts 4:32). This is the kind of love that was the hallmark of the early church, and it is this kind of unity that God himself is. Father, Son and Holy Spirit are three unique persons, but together they are one being. They may be three potatoes, but they cannot be separated, as their love has mashed them into one. This is a mystery; God is three, yet one. It is this kind of love that God also wants the church to be characterized by, a giving, selfless "mashed potato" love. A love that does not keep guard over what is mine but always strives to value others above oneself (Philippians 2:3).

The church is the community in which we realize our need for repentance, where we help one another find our own mature, growing faith. We rejoice together when, we through baptism, bury the old life and then we surround the new believers with prayer, praying that they will receive the Holy Spirit as a gift. After that, we walk side by side as fellow travelers on the way to salvation, ready to help and to be helped, "until we all reach unity in the faith and in the knowledge of the Son of God and become mature, attaining to the whole measure of the fullness of Christ" (Ephesians 4:13).

# Chapter 12

## DISCIPLES MAKING DISCIPLES

"Then the eleven disciples went to Galilee, to the mountain
where Jesus had told them to go. When they saw him, they
worshipped him; but some doubted. Then Jesus came to them
and said, all authority in heaven and on earth has been given to
me. Therefore go and make disciples of all nations, baptizing
them in the name of the Father and of the Son and of the Holy
Spirit, and teaching them to obey everything I have
commanded you. And surely I am with you always,
to the very end of the age."
Matthew 28:16–20

When I was about 15 years old, I found a book on my father's
bookshelf, a short book about Christian discipleship, packed
with quotes, stories and Bible verses. One of the quotes came
from Charles Thomas Studd, an English cricket player who
became a born-again Christian. He left a promising sports career
behind and became a missionary, traveling to Africa to talk
about the God he now knew. I can still remember reading the
quote of his, a quote that left me with a nagging feeling that I
had to live for something bigger than myself. I don't know
whether it came from a song or a sermon, but its words are
forever etched on my mind: "Some want to live within the sound
of church or chapel bell; I want to run a rescue shop within a
yard of hell." It is this kind of life that Jesus calls us to walk, a

life that leaves everlasting footprints behind us in this world, footprints that echo into eternity. The problem is that we all too often don't see or understand how important our small steps of in faith and obedience can be for the kingdom of God. When Jesus called his disciples, it was with a simple yet challenging call to follow him (Mark 1:16–20). They were a motley crowd of young men. Two of them Jesus called "sons of Thunder" (Mark 3:17), which probably reflected their temperament. There was doubting Thomas and Peter who made big promises without sticking to his words (Matthew 26:35). James and John argued over who would be seated at Jesus' right and left side in God's new kingdom (Mark 10:35-38). When we later read about Jesus' disciples in the book of Acts, we can see that they had undergone a striking transformation. I don't think any of them ever could have imagined what consequences Jesus would have on the way they lived their lives.

When Jesus gave his disciples the Great Commission, he told them to go into all the world and make disciples of all nations (Matthew 28:19–20), a mission that must have overwhelmed them. These eleven disciples were given the task of reaching the entire world. At best they knew Aramaic, some Hebrew and some Greek, but that did not stop them from going to preach in Persia, Egypt, Turkey, India and Ethiopia. According to the New Testament and the Church Fathers, all the disciples were persecuted for their faith, and some were even martyred for what they believed. They took Jesus' command very seriously and quite literally followed Him to the ends of the earth. They were willing to give their lives for the gospel of Jesus Christ. Church history tells us that they were shot with arrows, crucified, stoned, and even boiled alive.

## In the light of eternity

Jesus' disciples understood something that we all should understand: "Time is short. Eternity is long. It is only reasonable that this short life be lived in the light of eternity," as the preacher Charles Spurgeon said. When we read in the book of Acts about how the Jewish leaders questioned Peter and John, we are told that they considered them to be "unschooled, ordinary men" (Acts 4:13). The Greek words used here are *agrammatos* and *idiōtēs* which literally mean illiterates and idiots! It is a great encouragement that God can use people whom others look down on to bring an unimaginable change to the world. These apostles did not live to see the full fruits of their labors, all they got to see were a few small clusters of new disciples around the Mediterranean. However, they realized that the best way for them to live was to live for something bigger and better than life itself.

Now, thanks to two thousand years of hindsight, we can look back at all that God was able to accomplish through those disciples. We can marvel at what God can do through a small band of people who wholeheartedly live for Him. They followed Jesus to the end and walked ever more firmly in the faith that they had been taught. They burst through boundaries, crossed borders, and were willing to sacrifice their own lives for the One who is greater than life itself. Jesus transformed them and shaped the way they lived so that they were the salt of the earth and the light in the darkness (Matthew 5:13-14). Their lives and deeds testified as much to Jesus as did their words. The first apostles are an important reminder that God can use anyone He wants to build His kingdom. God's desire is that His church should be full of disciples who live to make new disciples. When Jesus commissioned His church to go out and make disciples, it came with a promise: "I will be with you always, to the very end of the age" (Matthew 28:20).

For God, nothing is impossible and there is no limit to what He can do through someone who places their life in His hands. God want us to become the men and women that He created us to be, not broken but forgiven, healed and whole. But even though we may be hurting, are broken and have a tendency to sin, God can still use us. The Bible is the amazing story of how God, through ordinary and simple people, brings forth his awesome plan. If we have set out to walk on God's narrow road, we cannot any longer follow our own hearts and desires. As followers of Christ, we shouldn't ask, "What are my dreams?" but rather, "What is God dreaming about?". We need to make sure that we are constantly walking as God wants with God's Holy Spirit as our guide. By walking His way, we will begin to understand that God really does have a plan for us, and that He is able to bring it to fruition.

In my youth, I once heard a preacher ask, "If you die tonight, where will you end up: heaven or hell?" I was terrified and thought, "I just have to go to heaven because I really don't want to go to hell." I have since come to realize that, although there is some truth to that question, it definitely has the wrong focus. The gospel is not a message about escaping death or even hell; rather, it is a message about life. A better question would be, "If you wake up tomorrow, what will you live for: God's eternal kingdom or your own temporary one?" It is only in the light of eternity that this short life on earth is supposed to be lived. There is more to life than we can see. The author C.S. Lewis has said,

"You can't go back and change the beginning, but you can start where you are and change the ending." If that is the case, then it is never too late to make a fresh start, nor is it too late to get a good start."

For those of us who have walked with Jesus for a long time, there may be a temptation to think that maturity and spiritual depth come from more study and greater knowledge. However, true maturity, and what truly deepens our faith, comes when we learn to seek His face and remain in Him. But not only that, it also happens when we choose to share with others what we ourselves have received. Serving, witnessing, and evangelizing are often the fastest ways to experience more of God's power, purpose, and joy, for in serving, we must learn to depend on Him. In the Christian faith, it is true that the one who gives the most is also the one who receives the most. The Christian walk is about becoming a disciple whose goal it is, to invite more people to follow Christ and become like Christ.

There is no limit to what God is able to do through a person who fully devotes himself to prayer and service to God. Prayer is the best way to see God's goodness and greatness. Unfortunately, too many people have a small view of God as someone who occasionally surpasses himself and in answering prayer. The truth is that we have a great God who is able to do far more than we can "ask or imagine" (Ephesians 3:20-31). God longs to answer our prayers, intervene in our lives, and transform our circumstances. Therefore, we need to repent and allow God to renew our minds so that we can see who He is and what He wants to do through us. If we truly understood the power of prayer than we would never stop getting down on our knees to pray. We should pray constantly and with a longing to see God's kingdom come and His will be done, "on earth as it is in heaven" (Matthew 6:10).

## DAY 36

## Who could ever imagine

In 1369, the Czech priest Jan Hus was born. He longed to see God at work in people's lives and therefore challenged some of the things he saw taking place in the Roman Catholic Church. Pretty soon he discovered that what he was trying to do wasn't as easy as he thought. He was put on trial and persecuted by the church, but nevertheless his ideas began to take a foothold, mainly among students in Prague. Sometime later Hus was invited to explain himself before the Pope in Rome. He went there in great enthusiasm, but it turned out to be a trap that ended with him being burned at the stake in 1415, aged 46. But what God had begun through him didn't end there. Many who had listened to Hus experienced God's love in a new way and held fast to his teachings. They were also persecuted and soon there was only a few of them left. Many years later they finally found sanctuary under the protection of the German Duke Nikolas Ludwig von Zinzendorf. He offered them a safe haven, and in 1722, Herrnhut (the Lord's Protection) was founded. Thus, the remnant of Jan Hus's followers finally found a refuge where they could live in peace and freely share their faith. There were of course divisions and conflicts among them, but one night, God spoke, and they chose to put all their fighting aside and repented as they were reconciled to each other, asking each other for forgiveness. The Spirit of God fell upon this gathering of repenting disciples, and they prayed, wept and embraced each other. They sang and worshiped the Lord and God intervened in a powerful way and touched them. The Spirit fell upon them just as on the day of Pentecost and God gave them a burning desire to evangelize the whole world. This was the start of a new era, where God again started to work through ordinary people who were filled with His Spirit. They sent out missionaries to Africa, Asia, Greenland and the West Indies. There are even stories of how some of their number sold themselves as slaves in order to preach about Jesus to their fellow slaves. They prayed and continued to pray, and that prayer meeting that begun in Herrnhut did not stop for over 100 years as they prayed, night and day, year after year.

In 1738, a disappointed and disillusioned Anglican missionary returned from the United States back to England. He wrote in his diary: "I went to America, to convert the Indians; but oh, who shall convert me?" During the voyages back home, a big storm blew up and everyone on the ship was scared, except for one German family which gathered around a table and sang to God. The missionary wondered what had kept them so calm in the midst of the raging storm. Their answer would forever echo in the Anglican missionary. They said: "We believe in Jesus so we know we will go to heaven if the ship sinks. And if it weathers the storm, we'll soon be back in England. So, we win no matter what." Once back in England that missionary, John Wesley, sought out that family and soon found himself in an evening revival meeting on Aldersgate Street in London. On the evening of 24 May1738 Wesley wrote in his diary:

> "In the evening I went very unwillingly to a society in Aldersgate Street, where one was reading Luther's preface to the Epistle to the Romans. About a quarter before nine, while he was describing the change which

God works in the heart through faith in Christ, I felt my heart strangely warmed. I felt I did trust in Christ, Christ alone, for salvation; and an assurance was given me that He had taken away my sins, even mine, and saved me from the law of sin and death. I began to pray with all my might for those who had in a more especial manner despitefully used me and persecuted me. I then testified openly to all there what I now first felt in my heart."

John Wesley became the leading figure in one of the most amazing revivals that has ever taken place and influenced the Christian church all over the world. The Methodist church that spang from it gave rise to new evangelical movements and later the charismatic movement that swept across the world from Azusa Street in 1906. I don't think Jan Hus could have imagined what the end result would be, but that's what God does: He has a habit of picking up nobodies and making them somebodies so they can be a blessing to anybody.

When I started as a pastor in Immanuel Church in Malmö in 2015 it was a year before the church celebrated its 150th anniversary. I decided to read through the history of the church and I was captivated by what I read. A priest named Efraim Bager was deeply influenced by the teachings of the Herrnhut movement and had visited Christiansfeld in Denmark, where the Herrnhut's had established a sanctuary. Upon returning to Malmö in the early 1860s, he founded a group for young men. This group became known as Bager's Youth Association. Through their Bible readings and prayers, they were moved by God's compassion for the lost and those living on the margins of society. This spiritual awakening led to the founding of Malmö's Evangelical Missionary Association in 1866, with the goal of making Jesus known not only in Malmö but also throughout the world. Just ten years later, this missionary association gave birth to Immanuel Church. I often remind myself that our church has its origins in a radical call to mission, wanting to lead people to Christ. And so, Jan Hus has also played a big part in my life as well, and I am eternally grateful for his dedication and willingness to serve God.

For God, nothing is impossible and there is no limit to what He can do through a person who places their life at His disposal. But if we want to walk as God desires, we cannot let our own hearts be our guide. We need to follow Jesus Christ wherever he leads. We need to make sure that we are constantly walking through life with him as our Lord. We need the Holy Spirit as our guide, then we will understand that God really has good works prepared for us to walk in (Ephesians 2:10).

Of all the hundreds of sermons that I have listened to, there is one by my friend Hans Jansson that I remember best. He told of an experience he had on the small Danish island of Bornholm. Walking along the beach one day, he noticed how he left footprints behind him in the wet sand. He said that when he eventually turned for home, he saw that several of his footprints had been erased by the waves, and at that moment a prayer was born in his heart: "God, don't let my life pass by without a trace; let me live my life so that I leave everlasting footprints behind me in this world." I remember that I cried when he said those words. I bowed my head and prayed, "That's how I want to live my life. I also want to leave everlasting footprints behind me in this world. I want to walk my life in such a way that my steps will echo into eternity."

# Praise to God for a Living Hope

Praise be to the God and Father of our Lord Jesus Christ!

In his great mercy he has given us new birth into a living
hope through the resurrection of Jesus Christ from the dead,
and into an inheritance that can never perish, spoil or fade.

This inheritance is kept in heaven for you, who through faith
are shielded by God's power until the coming of the
salvation that is ready to be revealed in the last time.

In all this you greatly rejoice, though now for a little while you
may have had to suffer grief in all kinds of trials. These have
come so that the proven genuineness of your faith
- of greater worth than gold,
which perishes even though refined by fire -
may result in praise, glory and honor when
Jesus Christ is revealed.

Though you have not seen him, you love him; and even though
you do not see him now, you believe in him and are filled with
an inexpressible and glorious joy, for you are receiving
the end result of your faith, the salvation of your souls.

1 Peter 1:3–9

# Appendix 1

A complete list of Bible words (NIV translation) where Paul uses the word *peripateō* (Strong's number G4043):

**Romans 6:4**
"We were therefore buried with him through baptism into death in order that, just as Christ was raised from the dead through the glory of the Father, we too may <u>live</u> (walk) a new life."

**Romans 8:1**
"Therefore, there is now no condemnation for those who <u>are</u> (walk) in Christ Jesus,"

**Romans 8:4**
"…in order that the righteous requirement of the law might be fully met in us, who do not <u>live</u> (walk) according to the flesh but according to the Spirit."

**Romans 13:13**
"Let us <u>behave</u> (walk) decently, as in the daytime, not in carousing and drunkenness, not in sexual immorality and debauchery, not in dissension and jealousy."

**Romans 14:15**
"If your brother or sister is distressed because of what you eat, you are no longer <u>acting</u> (walking) in love. Do not by your eating destroy someone for whom Christ died."

## 1 Corinthians 3:2–3

"I gave you milk, not solid food, for you were not yet ready for it. Indeed, you are still not ready. You are still worldly. For since there is jealousy and quarreling among you, are you not worldly? Are you not <u>acting</u> (walking) like mere humans?"

## 1 Corinthians 7:17

"Nevertheless, each person should <u>live</u> (walk) as a believer in whatever situation the Lord has assigned to them, just as God has called them. This is the rule I lay down in all the churches."

## 2 Corinthians 4:2

"Rather, we have renounced secret and shameful ways; we do not <u>use</u> (walk in) deception, nor do we distort the word of God. On the contrary, by setting forth the truth plainly we commend ourselves to everyone's conscience in the sight of God."

## 2 Corinthians 5:6–7

"Therefore we are always confident and know that as long as we are at home in the body we are away from the Lord. For we <u>live</u> (walk) by faith, not by sight."

## 2 Corinthians 10:2–3

"I beg you that when I come I may not have to be as bold as I expect to be toward some people who think that we <u>live</u> (walk) by the standards of this world. For though we <u>live</u> (walk) in the world, we do not wage war as the world does."

## 2 Corinthians 12:18

"I urged Titus to go to you and I sent our brother with him. Titus did not exploit you, did he? Did we not <u>walk</u> (walk) in the same footsteps by the same Spirit?"

**Galatians 5:16**

"So I say, walk (walk) by the Spirit, and you will not gratify the desires of the flesh."

**Ephesians 2:1–2**

"As for you, you were dead in your transgressions and sins, in which you used to live (walk) when you followed the ways of this world and of the ruler of the kingdom of the air, the spirit who is now at work in those who are disobedient."

**Ephesians 2:10**

"For we are God's handiwork, created in Christ Jesus to <u>do</u> (walk in) good works, which God prepared in advance for us to do."

**Ephesians 4:1**

"As a prisoner for the Lord, then, I urge you to <u>live</u> (walk) a life worthy of the calling you have received."

**Ephesians 4:17 (2 times)**

"So I tell you this, and insist on it in the Lord, that you must no longer live (walk) as the Gentiles do, in the futility of their thinking (walk)."

**Ephesians 5:1-2**

"Follow God's example, therefore, as dearly loved children ² and walk (walk) in the way of love, just as Christ loved us and gave himself up for us as a fragrant offering and sacrifice to God."

**Ephesians 5:8-9**

"For you were once darkness, but now you are light in the Lord. Live (walk) as children of light for the fruit of the light consists in all goodness, righteousness and truth."

### Ephesians 5:15

"Be very careful, then, how you live (walk), not as unwise but as wise…"

### Philippians 3:17

"Join together in following my example, brothers and sisters, and just as you have us as a model, keep your eyes on those who live (walk) as we do."

### Philippians 3:18

"For, as I have often told you before and now tell you again even with tears, many live (wanders) as enemies of the cross of Christ."

### Colossians 1:9–10

"We continually ask God to fill you with the knowledge of his will through all the wisdom and understanding that the Spirit gives, so that you may live (walk) a life worthy of the Lord and please him in every way: bearing fruit in every good work, growing in the knowledge of God…"

### Colossians 2:6–7

"So then, just as you received Christ Jesus as Lord, continue to live (walk) your lives in him, rooted and built up in him, strengthened in the faith as you were taught, and overflowing with thankfulness."

### Colossians 3:5–7

"Put to death, therefore, whatever belongs to your earthly nature: sexual immorality, impurity, lust, evil desires and greed, which is idolatry. Because of these, the wrath of God is coming. You used to walk in these ways, in the life you once lived."

## Colossians 4:5

"Be wise in the way you act (walk) toward outsiders; make the most of every opportunity."

## 1 Thessalonians 2:11–12

"For you know that we dealt with each of you as a father deals with his own children, [12] encouraging, comforting and urging you to live (walk) lives worthy of God, who calls you into his kingdom and glory."

## 1 Thessalonians 4:1

"As for other matters, brothers and sisters, we instructed you how to live in order to please God, as in fact you are living (walking). Now we ask you and urge you in the Lord Jesus to do this more and more."

## 1 Thessalonians 4:12

"...so that your daily life (walk) may win the respect of outsiders and so that you will not be dependent on anybody."

## 2 Thessalonians 3:6

"In the name of the Lord Jesus Christ, we command you, brothers and sisters, to keep away from every believer who is idle and disruptive and does not live (walk) according to the teaching You received from us."

# Thanks to...

Åsa, the love of my life, thank you for your patience and love. You are my best friend.

My beloved family, which is growing and growing with children and grandchildren.

Jonas Helgesson, without you – no book.

Hans Jansson, without you I would not be a pastor today.

Lasse Bjervås, who read and read and gave invaluable feedback.

David Pawson, we have a lot to talk about when we meet in the kingdom to come.

Hans Janson, Birgitta Sundin, Magnus Davidsson, Kim Brynte and others - colleagues who have shaped and sharpened me over the years.

My father Jörgen Ljung, your passion for seeing churches grow has been contagious.

Malcolm Searle, for doing an awesome job in helping me find the right English words. I couldn't have done it without you.